THE GRESLEY INFLUENCE

THE GRESLEY INFLUENCE

Geoffrey Hughes

B.Sc(Econ) C. Eng FIEE

LONDON

IAN ALLAN LTD

Cover: 'A4' No 4463 *Sparrow Hawk* on a
prewar express.

Previous page: Artists impression of the
proposed 4-8-2 of 1939. *Peter Winding*

First published 1983

ISBN 0 7110 1272 5

Published by Ian Allan Ltd, Shepperton, Surrey;
and printed by Ian Allan Printing Ltd at their works
at Coombelands in Runnymede, England

Contents

Foreword

by Lord Garnock

Sir Nigel Gresley's outstanding contribution to the development of the steam loco-motive has won him a unique place in the annals of locomotive engineering; his memory is revered by those who still recall the thrill of observing his locomotives in action, as well as by the ever growing numbers of enthusiasts to whom the days before railway nationalisation are a matter of history.

In this day and age of prototypes and seemingly endless bugs in any new piece of machinery, be it railway or otherwise, Gresley stands out in marked contrast, particularly over the amazing début of his 'A4' Pacifics and the 'Silver Jubilee'. Not only did *Silver Link* twice attain 112½mph and average 100mph for 43 miles continuously when only three weeks out of shops, but due to production delays at Doncaster, three days later No 2509 went into regular service on the 'Jubilee', working it exclusively for the first few weeks of service. This involved running 2,700 miles per week on a high-speed schedule the like of which had never hitherto been experienced.

When the honour of a knighthood was bestowed on Gresley in 1936, it was not for nothing that he was described by The Times as 'engineer and speeder-up to the LNER'.

Fortunately a number of his locomotives have been preserved, one of which, *The Great Marquess*, is amongst my proudest possessions. To enjoy the sight and sound of a Gresley engine in motion, and in particular to savour that unique three-cylinder exhaust beat, is to experience the best in the contemporary preservation scene. All this, of course, adds to the increasing interest in historical studies of the Gresley period.

Consequently, and particularly as President of the Gresley Society, I welcome this new book, which brings a fresh outlook to bear on Sir Nigel's personality and distinguished career, and on his wide influence on the British locomotive scene, discussing also several aspects of his engines previously unknown to those outside his immediate circle.

David Garnock

Introduction

More than any other piece of machinery, the steam locomotive epitomised the Industrial Revolution, providing the motive power of Britain's railways from the beginnings of the national system through to the virtual disappearance of steam from scheduled services in the 1960s. Depending upon one's viewpoint, the traditional steam locomotive was either shiny, glamourous and powerful, or dirty, noisy and inefficient, although in anybody's terms it was certainly a product of the best in heavy mechanical engineering. But in its classic form it was to find no place in the astringent world of the silicon chip, and its demise was inevitable in the advance of electric and diesel traction.

Throughout the century and a half during which the technology of the steam locomotive moved forward to achieve a degree of development totally beyond the vision of the early 19th century pioneers, many engineers contributed to the evolution of the locomotive. But amongst them were a small number who stood head and shoulders above their fellows, possessing not only outstanding engineering ability but also the confidence to move forward the technology as a whole, combining component innovation and improvement with dimensional increase. It is to the credit of these men, working within the constraints imposed by the processes of raising and using steam whilst on the move, that the steam locomotive reached its final stage of development.

The Great Northern was fortunate in possessing one of these engineers: the subject of this study, Nigel Gresley. Appointed Locomotive Engineer of the GNR in 1911 at the age of 35, Gresley spent his remaining 30 years with the Great Northern and its post-grouping successor, the London & North Eastern Railway, introducing a series of locomotives renowned both for their performance and their elegance. His influence on design ranged from improvements to the engines of his predecessor H. A. Ivatt to the greater part of the locomotives produced by his LNER successors, and can be traced in important features of the final steam design for British Railways, the *Duke of Gloucester*.

A number of parallel paths of experimentation and development can be followed through the years of Gresley's career as a chief mechanical engineer, and of those who followed him; consequently, apart from the brief sketch in chapter 2, I have not followed the conventional path of taking the whole of his work in strictly chronological order. Chapters 3 to 9 deal with particular groups of locomotives, and chapters 10 to 12 discuss his work on particular components of the total design. Some overlap has been unavoidable, but this is no more than is necessary to preserve continuity when following a particular path.

In the text, locomotives are generally identified by their running numbers and classes used during the prewar LNER period. When there are exceptions, these are made clear. It is regretted that reasons of space preclude any reference to Gresley's many achievements in the carriage and wagon field.

It is not the purpose of this book to present a comprehensive biography of Nigel Gresley, nor to deal in minute detail with the individual design of his locomotives, and especially not to feature tables of performance. These topics are adequately dealt with in other books mentioned in the Bibliography. Instead, in the context of the contemporary railway environment, and the personalities surrounding him, I offer a portrait of the man and his engines.

Geoff Hughes
Chorley Wood
1982

Chapter 1

Nigel Gresley: Chief Mechanical Engineer

Herbert Nigel Gresley was born in Dublin Street, Edinburgh, on 19 June 1876, the fifth child of the Rev Nigel Gresley, rector of Netherseal, in Derbyshire. His forbears were country gentry, and no family influence existed to attract him into a career as an engineer. Unlike some of his contemporaries, he did not marry into an engineering family, nor did any of his four children achieve eminence in the profession. From the age of 14, until he left at 17, he was educated at Marlborough, traditionally a school for sons of clergymen, where there is no strong engineering bias, and the reasons for his motivation towards locomotive engineering are not immediately obvious. However his family are convinced that the railway bug first bit during his boyhood, when watching local trains in the vicinity of Netherseal. This is also the conclusion of his biographer, F. A. S. Brown, who also believes that when at Marlborough the young Gresley may have been attracted by the Gooch Single-drivers running on the Great Western main line nearby. Whether in those days his ambition was to become a locomotive engineer but without any specific railway in mind also cannot be known for certain, but he has left one piece of evidence that he had some partiality for the Great Northern. When he was about 15 he made a detailed tracing from a large drawing in *The Engineer* of a Stirling 7ft 6in Single built a few years earlier. One wonders whether he drew others, but if so none have been preserved nor have any less detailed outlines he may have sketched during his schooldays. However many later drawings made in his years in training have survived and these display an excellent standard of draughtsmanship, remaining as sharp as if they had been drawn yesterday.

Clearly Gresley had made up his mind about his future before he left Marlborough, and he wasted no time in seeking a position with a major railway, preferring the real world of engineering to a period in the Sixth Form at school. Often in those days a personal introduction was necessary to obtain a mechanical engineering apprenticeship, and if his leanings were in fact towards the GNR, he was evidently unsuccessful in an approach to Patrick Stirling. Anyway, in 1893 he was accepted as a premium apprentice under Francis Webb at Crewe, and his initial years as a railwayman were spent on the London & North Western, where he worked assiduously to gain experience of locomotive design, construction and operation, remaining at Crewe for a year as a fitter, after completing his apprenticeship. Next, in 1898, he secured a junior position with the Lancashire & Yorkshire at Horwich, in the design office of J. A. F. (later Sir John) Aspinall, after a while taking charge of the materials test room before moving to the operational field when he became for a time running shed foreman at Blackpool. The year 1900 saw him enter the Carriage & Wagon side of the L&Y, becoming successively Outdoor Assistant to the C&W Superintendent, Assistant Manager and then Manager of the C&W works at Newton Heath, and finally in 1904, Assistant Superintendent of the Carriage & Wagon Department. A year later, not yet 30, he moved to Doncaster as Carriage & Wagon Superintendent under H. A. Ivatt, himself a Crewe trained engineer, to succeed E. F. Howlden, who had been in charge of the development and construction of GNR coaching stock since Stirling had appointed him in 1877, and who had left a solid legacy of bogie coaches with clerestory roofs on American lines, many of which were to survive well into LNER days.

The circumstances of Gresley's move to Doncaster suggest that he was Ivatt's personal choice, if not, initially, that of the GNR Board. The vacancy was advertised, and six other applicants were interviewed by a panel of Directors without an appointment being made. Later it was announced that Ivatt had arranged for Gresley to take over Howlden's post at a salary of £750, which was 'not to be considered final if his work justifies more'. Ivatt was a close friend of Aspinall, who undoubtedly had been impressed by Gresley's ability and who must have spoken well on his behalf. One of the unsuccessful applicants was Francis Wintour, who had also transferred from the L&Y to the Great Northern, as Locomotive Running Superintendent at Kings Cross, in 1902. Possibly Gresley's greater experience in the C&W field was a telling point in his favour; as it happened, following D. Earle Marsh's move to the LBSC, Wintour was appointed Locomotive Works Manager at Doncaster at the same time as Gresley joined the Great Northern.

Although reporting to Ivatt as a senior member of his Department, Gresley was given a good deal of freedom by his Chief — more perhaps than in later years Gresley was to allow his own subordinates. Very soon he was to implant his own refinement on Howlden's coach outline by introducing an elliptical roof which, with the traditional varnished teak bodywork, was to form the familiar pattern of East Coast coaching stock until special finishes began to be introduced in the 1930s. When, in 1911, Ivatt elected to retire, there was no doubt in the minds of the Great Northern Board that they need look no further for his successor than their 35-year old Carriage & Wagon Superintendent. So, at a commencing salary of £1,800, Gresley was appointed Locomotive Engineer on 1 October 1911, responsible for the efficient condition of the company's locomotive, carriage and wagon departments, of machinery at stations and depots, and of all road and other vehicles used by the company. He was allowed to take a limited number of pupils on a personal basis. His office remained at Doncaster, convenient for the design office and the Plant, but 156 miles away from the GNR Head Office at Kings Cross. This tended to emphasise the independence that characterised Gresley's career, which led on occasion to slightly strained relations with his superiors, and which without sympathetic handling by members of the Board, and generosity on Gresley's part when it was most needed, could have led to difficulties.

On moving into Ivatt's chair, Gresley inherited an organisation in which Wintour continued as Locomotive Works Manager, and who would have considered favourably his own qualifications for the top post, possibly resenting the appointment of the younger Gresley. However, whatever Wintour's private thoughts may have been, there was no lasting rancour, and the new Locomotive Engineer quickly settled into his job, demonstrating that he was determined to maintain the Great Northern's position amongst the leaders of locomotive development. Another who was to be associated with him from the earliest days was Oliver Bulleid, who in later years became Gresley's close confidant, until Bulleid himself became Chief Mechanical Engineer of the Southern Railway in 1937. Bulleid provides an interesting insight into Gresley's relations with Charles Dent, the GNR General Manager. In response to a somewhat critical letter from Dent, Bulleid drafted an apologetic explanation, but Gresley would have none of this. Refusing to express regret, he ignored the main import of the letter, concentrating on a minor point. 'That's the way to deal with such matters', he told Bulleid.

In the remaining years of the Great Northern's independent existence, before it was to lose its identity at the grouping, Gresley gained steadily in reputation with a sequence of new and important designs. He might confidently have expected to be chosen to take charge of the locomotive department of the new East Coast group, but this was by no means a certainty.

Following the provisions of the 1921 Railways Act, which established the four main railway groups on 1 January 1923, but which left them still in private ownership and with the freedom to organise themselves as they saw fit, the formative period of the LNER was one of considerable manoeuvring amongst the Directors of the constituent companies to protect the interests of their own particular lines. The Great Central, Great Eastern, Great Northern and North British, probably saw in the grouping their main hope for a reasonably prosperous future — indeed the first three had projected their own scheme of amalgamation before the war, but this had been turned down by the Government of the day. The Great North of Scotland would probably have preferred continued independent penury to the prospect of becoming the remote end of an attenuated system based on far-off London, whilst the North Eastern, still earning substantial revenues from hauling coal from the pits to the docks for export, were anxious to ensure that their relative prosperity should not be eroded in favour of propping up the less profitable lines. In unofficial pre-grouping discussions, the NER naturally had the loudest voice, although their Chairman, Lord Knaresborough, was not the most forceful of personalties, and neither he nor the Great Northern Chairman, Sir Frederick Banbury, both in their late 70s, wanted to take a leading part in running the new group. In the event, William Whitelaw, grandfather of the present William Whitelaw, who had been Chairman of the North British for 10 years, as well as having held the similar post on the Highland Railway, was elected Chairman of the LNER Board. Not, it is probable, without a strong case having been put forward on behalf of Lord Faringdon, of the Great Central, but in the event Faringdon became LNER Deputy Chairman, and a close working relationship soon grew up between the two. The Board was constituted by no fewer than 26 members, appointed in a proportion representing the interests of the constituent companies, but according to a formula only arrived at after long negotiation.

A key position in the new group was that of General Manager — or, rather, since it was decided early on that a decentralised Area organisation was to be introduced — Chief General Manager, whose job would be to weld the disparate constituents into a coherent whole, and to run the railway under the general direction of the Board. A strong contender for this position was the formidable Sir Eric Geddes, who in prewar days had made a meteoric rise within the NER to become Deputy General Manager with the understanding that he would eventually succeed Sir Alexander Butterworth as General Manager. However he had been seconded to the Government during the war, becoming Minister of Transport in 1919, after the NER had paid him £50,000 in consideration of severance of his contract. It seems to have been no secret that Geddes would have relished the opportunity to return to railway service as Chief General Manager (or even Chairman or Managing Director) of the LNER, and actively canvassed his claim, but he had alienated the North Eastern Board, and they had by now a desire to appoint anyone but Geddes. Nevertheless, in a curious circumlocutory way Faringdon was thought to have supported Geddes' claim — possibly as a device which would allow the North Eastern to have appeared to have provided the General Manager, but by one who had had his mind broadened by an absence of several years on other duties. In the meantime, however, with the twin objectives of ensuring continued NER leadership but appointing someone other than Geddes, Sir Alexander Butterworth visualised that at his age (67) he would not be unanimously supported for the CGM's job, and offered the suggestion that he should stand down as North Eastern General Manager in favour of his Deputy, Ralph Wedgwood. The NER Board acceded to this, and consequently appointed Wedgwood as General Manager at the beginning of 1922, giving him a year in the saddle, sufficient to bring him the seniority and experience needed to press his claim to become the Chief General Manager of the LNER. Butterworth stayed with the North Eastern as a consultant, and this position enabled him to work freely behind the scenes for the benefit of the NER, in the pre-amalgamation discussions.

Amongst the other General Managers of the East Coast constituent companies, there were some formidable figures. Sir Henry Thornton, the American highflyer who had taken charge of the Great Eastern as the request of Lord Claud Hamilton had already decided to return across the Atlantic to take up the management of Canadian National Railways. Of the others, Sir Sam Fay of the Great Central would be 65 in 1923, and Charles Dent of the Great Northern only a year or two younger. James Calder, the North British incumbent, was 52, but he had no desire to leave Scotland; he remained with the LNER as General Manager (Scotland) until his retirement in 1934. Ralph Wedgwood, then, was the obvious choice, being the right age and possessing the right experience, and this is how it was seen by the Organising Committee — a group of Directors set up to establish the management guidelines of the new company — who, at their meeting on 25 October 1922 arranged for the appointment of Wedgwood as Chief General Manager, this being confirmed at the first formal meeting of the new LNER Board. As well as Wedgwood, the North Eastern also provided the Chief Legal Adviser, Sir Francis Dunnell; Sir Sam Fay remained for a year, 'at the disposal of the CGM', and Dent retired.

However no such urgency surrounded the appointment of the Locomotive Engineer — now to be designated Chief Mechanical Engineer — of the group, and

January 1923 passed without an announcement being made. In addition to Gresley, the possible candidates were Sir Vincent Raven (North Eastern), J. G. Robinson (Great Central), A. J. Hill (Great Eastern), W. Chalmers (North British) and T. E. Heywood (Great North of Scotland). Of these, Chalmers and Heywood were hardly of the stature or experience the position demanded, whilst Hill decided to accept the terms proferred by the Railways Act, and retire. At the time, Raven was 63 and Robinson 66, but in those days retirement was not automatic at 65 or indeed at any age. Unless there was pressure from the Board, a Chief Officer might carry on until he elected to retire, and Robinson for one would have been happy to do so.

During the latter part of 1922, frequent meetings were held between the Locomotive Engineers, not so much concerned with locomotive matters as with identifying topics which needed inter-line standardisation, such as braking systems, corridor connections, and renumbering of rolling stock. One other subject was the ascertainment of the capability of the several workshops of the new group for construction and repair of locomotives, coaches and wagons. These meetings were chaired by Raven, who called the first one by saying that 'his General Manager (ie Wedgwood, the CGM designate) had asked him to call together the mechanical engineers'. Presumably as CME of the dominant partner in the group he was accepted by the others as their senior. All the Locomotive Engineers generally attended these meetings except Robinson, who sometimes sent his assistant, R. A. Thom, evidently with the instruction to contribute to the effect that 'the Great Central does it this way and there is no point in changing'. However with an NER man as Chief General Manager, it would have been asking a lot of the other railways to accept Raven as CME. Moreover, whilst Raven, in succeeding the Worsdells, had generally maintained a tradition of straightforward locomotives adequate for the tasks set them, his prestige Pacific was little more than an elongated 'Z' class Atlantic, hurried into service in a late effort to demonstrate that the North Eastern could build a really big engine. In his late 60s, Robinson would have found the prospect of tackling the locomotive problems of the new railway almost overwhelming, possessed of great heart though he was. He had produced a stud of locomotives which, in the 'Directors' and 2-8-0s included masterpieces, but his curious sequence of 4-6-0s were noted more for their capability for hard slogging than for their efficiency, and lacked any obvious coherence in design. But Gresley's Pacific of 1922, painstakingly developed on the drawing board over several years, was clearly a step forward into a new and exciting era, technically much in advance of any design of Raven or Robinson.

Undoubtedly Gresley's ability and his record would have impressed any impartial observer; indeed he would have been seen to lead the field by a large margin. But of course, as is so often the case, not all of those in whose hands lay the choice of the CME were impartial. Despite the fact that their choice would have meant a change before many years had passed, North Eastern interests plumped for Raven, and Lord Faringdon would have chosen Robinson, with whom he had worked so closely on the Great Central. Discussions took place, privately, and it was not until 22 February 1923, almost two months after the grouping, that the decision was taken by the Locomotive Committee that Gresley should be appointed CME at an annual salary of £4,500, and this was confirmed by the Board the following day. Raven, who meanwhile had simplified the issue by intimating his intention to retire (he had joined the board of Metropolitan Vickers) was given a year's appointment as Technical Adviser, at his NER salary of £4,000. He was asked firstly to report on the management of the Locomotive Running Department, and then on the best manner of utilising the workshops of the constituent companies, a topic on which the Mechanical Engineers had already held discussions. These tasks he tackled with expedition, submitting an excellent assessment of the position in each case, with recommendations which were largely accepted. Later in 1923 he was concerned with proposals for electrification of the GN suburban system, for which purpose a technical committee was set up, Raven being the chairman and Gresley a member. Robinson was also retained as a Consultant until the end of 1923, but there is no record of his having been asked to carry out any specific tasks. Interestingly the Raven, and particularly the Robinson, styles, were perpetuated in new locomotive construction by Gresley in the years following the grouping.

In a letter to the *Railway Gazette* published just after Gresley's death in April 1941, Robinson claimed to have been offered the CME's position, but that he had declined this and had recommended Gresley for the post. Perhaps what is more probable is that Faringdon would have promised Robinson to do what he could, but in the event a majority of Directors favoured Gresley. The case would then have been put gently to Robinson, that, having regard to all the circumstances, would he not agree that Gresley was the best choice? E. D. Trask, who later achieved eminence as Motive Power Superintendent of Eastern and North Eastern Regions of British Railways, and who was then a mechanical engineer on Gresley's staff, recalled that in February 1923 he had just completed the paperwork surrounding the repurchase from the War Department of two tank engines which had been armour plated for defence purposes. The forms needed the signature of the CME, and he went to the appropriate office to secure this, not knowing who in fact would be the signatory. He was told to wait outside the Board Room. In the corridor he met Gresley, who told him that there was no CME at the moment but if he waited he might find out. Eventually he saw Robinson emerge and walk away; Gresley was called in, and shortly afterwards came out grinning broadly. 'Now give me that form' he said to Trask.

So, in 1923, the second half of Nigel Gresley's career in engineering management commenced. The first 18 years with the Great Northern, culminating with his impressive Pacifics, were preparation for the second period, also of 18 years, when his locomotives gained such prestige for the LNER, the engineering profession, and for himself.

The LNER organisation was soon established, on paper at least. Under the CGM in London, three Areas were identified, each with a Divisional General Manager responsible for running the railway in his Area. (In passing, it is difficult for the historian to understand why the geographical title should have been 'Area', and the job title 'Divisional'. One or other would have covered both. This was a mystery even to senior LNER officers.) The largest Area was the Southern Area, an amalgamation of the physically quite separate Great Central, Great Eastern and Great Northern. S. A. Parnwell, Thornton's successor on the GER, became Divisional General Manager, Southern Area, at grouping, but for a year only, being succeeded by Alex Wilson, who had been Wedgwood's deputy for the last 12 months of the North Eastern's independent existence and who under the

LNER had initially taken on the post of Divisional General Manager, North Eastern Area. So, the erstwhile Great Northern was managed first by a Great Eastern man, and then by one from the North East. Such was the policy of the new company, to move its senior officers round on promotion, so minimising the retention of old loyalties, as well as, hopefully, putting the best men where they were most needed. Possibly the unweildy Southern Area proved difficult to manage efficiently. In 1926 the Board was concerned about the 'great waste due to delays to traffic', whilst the following year matters came to a head in the Great Eastern section, when growing operational difficulties led to a proposal that the Southern Area should be divided into two Areas, each with a Divisional General Manager. However the management situation was resolved at less expense by retaining the one Area, but appointing two Superintendents to manage the running of the railway, one for the Eastern Section (Great Eastern) and one for the Western Section (Great Central and Great Northern), each reporting to the Southern Area Divisional General Manager.

Of the remainder of the LNER, the North Eastern Area remained effectively the area of the NER, whilst the North British and the Great North of Scotland were merged into the Scottish Area, although for a time certain responsibilities were divided into the Southern Scottish (NB) and Northern Scottish (GNofS) Areas.

Not all powers were delegated to the Areas, and naturally enough the main streams of Accountancy and Secretarial matters were centred under the Chief General Manager in London, together with industrial relations, Parliamentary matters, and press, public relations and advertising so far as they affected the railway as a whole. The post of Chief Mechanical Engineer was one of the few all-line positions, the CME being responsible for construction and overhaul of rolling stock for the entire system. Civil Engineering was for many years delegated to the Areas, with no strong central direction, and not until the stress of the war years in 1942 was an all-line Civil Engineer appointed, in the person of J. C. L. (later Sir Landale) Train. In the same year an overall operating manager was appointed, V. M. (later Sir Michael) Barrington-Ward.

To guide the Chief General Manager on matters of policy, the Board established a number of Committees of Directors to give consideration to departmental and other aspects of the business, as for example Committees dealing with Traffic, Organisation, and Locomotive matters. The Locomotive Committee was the CME's Departmental Committee, considering matters both of Board policy and of detailed items of expenditure, strangely occupying itself to a much greater extent with the minutae of replacement machinery in the works and the finalisation of details of electricity and water supplies, than to the locomotives themselves, or other rolling stock. All Committee Minutes and recommendations went to the full Board, which reserved to itself the final decisions in major matters. Locomotive requirements in the Areas were made known in general terms upwards to the Divisional General Managers, who considered them in the light of Area operating costs and forwarded them to the CME, at which level an increasingly questioning survey was conducted. Informal talks would establish which locomotive classes would best meet traffic needs, and the pattern became established for a locomotive building programme to be put before a joint meeting of the Locomotive and Traffic Committees each November, for implementation during the following year. Almost invariably (but there was the occasional exception, as in 1927 when it reduced to 10 a proposal to build 20 4-6-0s of an obsolescent Great Eastern design) the meeting would accept the recommendations put to it, and these would be endorsed by the Board. The shortness of time between the authority to proceed with a programme, and its commencement, indicates that often the officers pre-empted the Board's decision, or programmes ran late. There never seemed to be any attempt to establish a longer term strategy, whilst in the rapidly worsening financial state of the company in the early 1930s changes and cancellations of parts of the programme inevitably occurred.

These led to a position in which the numbers and types of locomotives built in any one year always differed from the schedule in the approved programme. In the aftermath of the depression, in 1933, only 17 new locomotives were added to stock, but after this the numbers increased, aided by low-interest funds provided by the Government, but the company's situation was never sufficiently profitable to allow the CME a free hand to scrap and replace, until Government money was again available after the war, this time in recompense for revenues earned during the period in which the railways had been under Government control. Instead, selected classes of secondary locomotives were the subject of modernisation, this sometimes taking the form of partial or complete rebuilding on Gresley lines. Few of these were the subject of report to the Locomotive Committee, which indicates the free hand Gresley enjoyed in certain directions, whilst being severely restricted in others. All new construction had to be approved in detail, and the CME was permitted to spend no more than £200 on individual items of new capital equipment without obtaining authority, yet repairs and even major renewals carried out in workshops were subjected only to an overall financial control, governed roughly by the capability of the workshops in terms of resources. Gresley's greatest achievement, as an example of what he could get away with without reporting officially to the Board, was his massive 'Hush-Hush' experimental locomotive, No 10000, which was never the subject of inclusion in a building programme or other formal approval.

Andrew K. McCosh, who had occupied a similar position on the North British, following his father on to the Board, succeeded Bernard Firth of the Great Northern as Chairman of the Locomotive Committee in 1929. McCosh, an astute Scot with mining and engineering interests, had obtained a mechanical engineering tripos at Cambridge, and could discuss technicalities with Gresley; a warm friendship developed between them. No doubt McCosh, and Firth before him, were Gresley's confidants on important matters which for one reason or another did not reach the Board. Gresley got on well, too, with his Chairman, William Whitelaw, who in earlier years on the Highland Railway had had to part company with his Locomotive Engineer, F. G. Smith, for failing to consult the Civil Engineer over the weight of a new class of 4-6-0.

The Locomotive Committee was Gresley's main formal avenue of contact with his Directors, but he was almost at arm's length from them in that major Papers to the Committee, including locomotive building proposals, were not in his name, but in that of the Chief General Manager. Occasionally Gresley would submit a memorandum on a particular subject, but this would be initialled by Wedgwood. At meetings of the Locomotive Committee he would often be accompanied by a specialist assistant or two, depending upon what was on the agenda, whilst the

Area Locomotive Running Superintendents would also be present. Normally, the CME did not attend full meetings of the Board, the Officers present being the Chief General Manager, the Secretary, and the Chief Legal Adviser; Gresley did attend however when matters of importance specific to his Department were discussed, as for example the annual locomotive building programme.

The establishment which came within the ambit of the new CME at the grouping in 1923, was considerable by contemporary standards. The LNER inherited over 7,400 locomotives, almost entirely steam, with a few electric locomotives and petrol engined railcars, and some 20,000 coaches and 300,000 wagons. A staff of 103,000 worked in the design offices and the construction and repair shops at Darlington, York, Shildon and Hull (NER), Doncaster (GNR), Gorton and Dukinfield (GCR), Stratford (GER), Cowlairs (NBR), Inverurie (GNofS) and other smaller locations. Raven's report on the condition and capability of the workshops must have been invaluable to Gresley, and an early start was made on rationalisation, a process which continued throughout the LNER's existence, although at nothing like the pace which has characterised similar activitives in more recent years. The duties of the CME of course embraced far more than the design, construction and overhaul of rolling stock, although this is regarded by observers as the most important aspect of his work. Whilst the Civil Engineer was responsible for the permanent way, buildings, bridges and signalling, the CME had to provide and maintain electricity, gas and water supplies wherever they were needed, as well as all the machinery in workshops and depots, and the outside machinery in places such as pumping stations and coaling plants, involving a host of major and minor technical matters. Each year he was required to certify that the fixed and moving machinery in his care was in a fit state of repair to undertake the work it was called upon to do. He was also responsible for road motors and later on, for docks machinery. Nothing which moved was too large or too small for the CME. One of the smallest vehicles he was called upon to design was a refreshment trolley for platform use. 'What a thing to ask the CME to do' said Gresley. An important additional post was created in 1930 by the appointment as Chief Chemist and Metallurgist of T. Henry Turner, who rendered invaluable assistance to the CME on his specialist subjects, particularly water softening.

The CME's headquarters staff was miniscule by today's standards. Transferring his office from Doncaster to Kings Cross, overlooking the old main departure platform 10, Gresley worked with a small personal staff of whom the senior was Oliver Bulleid, dealing with special projects and outstationed staff, succeeded later by D. R. Edge. Bert Spencer was there as technical assistant on locomotive design, and Frank Day, succeeded by Norman Newsome, as carriage and wagon assistant. The Electrical Engineer was H. W. H. Richards, who came from the LBSC in 1924, and there was a small clerical staff. No such positions existed, as one might expect to see today, of Director of Design, or Director of Construction. At no time did Gresley have a designated Deputy, or an assistant with overall control of the workshops. This reflected the management policy of the LNER, dictated by cost as well as by practice, to reduce the strength of headquarters staff to the absolute minimum. Organisationally the Chief Mechanical Engineer delegated authority to Mechanical Engineers in the Areas, although the territory covered and the title varied from time to time. The duties of the Mechanical Engineers were primarily to represent the CME in two-way communication with the Operating Department, and to exercise general supervision over the Works Managers of the Locomotive, and the Carriage and Wagon Works, located in their territory, as well as being responsible for outdoor machinery. On occasion a Mechanical Engineer or Works Manager would originate certain specialised work, examples of which are seen in Edward Thompson's rebuilding of the Great Eastern 4-6-0s, initiated in 1932 when he was at Stratford, and in J. F. Harrison's thoroughgoing reorganisation of locomotive overhaul at Gorton and later in Scotland.

In common with the majority of pre-grouping railways, the Great Northern arranged for their Locomotive Engineer to have the responsibility for locomotive running, as well as for construction and overhaul. However, following another of Raven's recommendations, as Technical Adviser, the LNER decided to remove this function from the CME and decentralise it to the Divisional General Managers. A Locomotive Running Superintendent was appointed in each Area, responsible for organising and maintaining the Area stock of locomotives, apart from major overhauls, for which the engines would be sent to the main Works. But provision of plant in the running sheds remained within the purview of the CME, and inevitably financial stringency had its repercussions in the sheds, which were at the bottom of the list so far as new machinery was concerned, and often had to be satisfied with secondhand plant displaced from the Works. Locomotive crews did not work directly for the CME, nor originally, did the Locomotive Running Superintendents; however many of the engineers concerned with locomotive running had been trained at Doncaster and were well acquainted with Gresley. The system was revised when trial arrangements were introduced into the Southern Area in 1938, under which the Locomotive Running Superintendents' duties were defined in a dichotomy under which they were responsible to the Divisional General Manager for locomotive working, and to the CME for the mechanical repair of the engines in their charge. This was evidently a satisfactory arrangement, as it was later extended to the entire railway.

Never during its entire existence did the LNER have an all-line Commercial Manager, let alone a Director of Marketing, responsibility for obtaining business being in the hands of Passenger Managers and Goods Managers in the Areas. Insofar as anyone injected new commercial ideas into the railway, it was the CGM, Ralph Wedgwood, created KBE a year after his appointment. It was he who was primarily responsible for introducing a number of profitable developments, including lower prices for monthly return tickets, and the introduction of the first streamline service, the 'Silver Jubilee', in 1935. Wedgwood was regarded as a brilliant administrator, and much of the credit for welding the LNER into an entity must be his, as well as the constant vigilance on methods of cost saving, often severe, in efforts to keep the railway solvent. Moreover he was noted for his skill as an advocate in arguing the railway's case before Parliamentary Committees, particularly during the Square Deal campaign of the 1930s.

Wedgwood's senior assistant was Robert Bell, a Scot who had accompanied his chief from the North Eastern. As an important part of his duties, Bell had to keep a close eye on staff salaries, and all pay increases to staff in salaried grades had to be approved by him. These were always minimal, and his attitude, inevitably influenced by the chronic cash shortage of the company, was understandably negative. When a larger rise than usual was proposed for any individual, his response was to ask who should have his salary reduced to compensate for this? Indeed, it has been said that once, when Wedgwood told him to award himself a rise, he refused, saying that the company couldn't afford it. J. F. Harrison recalled that when Gresley wanted him to move to Gorton in 1930, he was offered a rise from £375 to £450. 'I'll just go and clear it with Mr Bell,' said Gresley. But he returned looking crestfallen. 'Mr Bell tells me that you had a £25 rise last year' he said. 'You can only have £400.'

A feature of the staff structure of those days was the extraordinary steepness of the salary pyramid, with for the topmost position, a quite phenomenal salary, unaffected by the financial performance of the company. (Except that in the depths of the depression everyone from the Chairman down took a 5% cut in remuneration, restored after a while in two $2\frac{1}{2}$% stages.) The salary of the Chief General Manager was fixed in 1923 at £10,000 a year, the next highest paid officer being Sir Francis Dunnell, the Chief Legal Adviser, who was on £7,000. The Chief Mechanical Engineer was paid £4,500, and the Divisional General Managers £3,500 to £5,000. This was at a time when the typical Station Master would be paid £350 to £500, and an unskilled workman's basic pay was £2.10p a week.

A more positive activity of Robert Bell's was masterminding the concept of 'traffic apprentice'. This exercise in management training which originated in the NER brought into the Company non-technical graduates and young men from public schools and offered similar opportunities through competitive examination to members of the administrative and clerical staff. Bell continued to oversee the programme in LNER days, and it is a tribute to the selection and training, as well as to the calibre of the individuals concerned, that at nationalisation no fewer than five of the top posts in the British Transport Commission and the Railway Executive went to men who had been LNER traffic apprentices. Later, in the person of Sir Henry Johnson, another traffic apprentice became Chairman of the British Railways Board, one of the very few railwaymen who made it to the very top. Equally was the influence in other spheres of British Railways of engineers who had trained under Gresley, particularly J. F. Harrison, who would have become CME of the LNER had it continued its independent existence, and who became instead Chief Engineer (Traction and Rolling Stock) of British Railways, and T. C. B. Miller, who also rose to this position, continuing when it was redesignated Chief Mechanical and Electrical Engineer (CMEE). A. H. Emerson, one of only three LNER premium apprentices whose training included both mechanical and electrical engineering, and whose father had been District Locomotive Running Superintendent at Grantham and Peterborough, became CMEE of the London Midland Region, and had the particular pleasure, for an LNER man, of electrifying the West Coast main line. R. A. Smeddle and T. Matthewson-Dick became successive CMEE's of the Western Region, Matthewson-Dick achieving Acting General Manager before retiring, whilst H. H. Swift, the LNER Assistant Electrical Engineer, followed in Bulleid's footsteps to become CMEE of the Southern Region.

Gresley's talents and effort received official recognition in 1936, when he was created Knight Bachelor, becoming Sir Nigel Gresley. He sadly passed away unexpectedly in his 65 year, on 5 April 1941, although his health had not been of the best for some time. He was succeeded by Edward Thompson until the end of June 1946, when Arthur Peppercorn took over the CME's chair. William Whitelaw had retired from the Board in 1938, being followed as Chairman by Sir Ronald Matthews; the Chief General Manager, Sir Ralph Wedgwood, had retired in 1939, to be succeeded by C. H. (later Sir Charles) Newton, who in turn just before nationalisation, gave way to Miles Beevor. So, for virtually the whole of his service on the LNER, Gresley worked under one Chairman, William Whitelaw, and one Chief General Manager, Sir Ralph Wedgwood. During this period, despite the restrictions imposed by the LNER's financial position, the company's locomotive stock was in general maintained in satisfactory condition. The decline in traffic which led to loss of revenue meant of course less demand on the locomotive stock, so that the rate of scrapping of old locomotives could exceed the rate of construction of new ones. Nevertheless, had the money been available, a greater rate of replacement would have been achieved, but whereas on the Great Western and the LMS, substantial construction of mixed traffic 4-6-0s took place in the 1930s, to replace older low-powered locomotives, Gresley was unable to follow suit, and it was not until cash was available at the end of the war and many engines literally on their last legs, that Thompson was able to initiate a programme of scrap and replace. Consequently it is a matter of great credit to Gresley and his staff, and to all concerned in locomotive running, that the older engines were kept going. Apart from major rebuilding in selected cases, the general attitude was one of repair as before, although some attempt was made to standardise minor components such as buffers and boiler mountings.

Sir Nigel Gresley's swan song was his 2-6-2 *Bantam Cock*, which packed all his design characteristics into a punchy, go-anywhere locomotive which could have been the forerunner of a large fleet, to replace many ageing pre-grouping engines. But the timing was inopportune: in wartime, emphasis was on greater simplicity and standardisation, and this was the course followed by his successor.

Chapter 2

GNR and LNER Locomotive Development

Nigel Gresley's initial priority on assuming office in October 1911 was clear. Ivatt had provided a sound fleet of locomotives to meet all requirements except for fast freight, and a larger class of locomotive was required to handle this growing traffic, as well as to meet demands for excursion and relief passenger working. So, a new mixed traffic type was the locomotive to which Gresley turned his attention at the outset. No doubt he had been attracted by the merits of the 2-6-0 wheel arrangement, with its pony truck offering better riding at speed than the 0-6-0, as well as the facility for a larger boiler and outside cylinders, by reports brought back by H. Holcroft following his visit to the United States in 1909. Holcroft was then working for G. J. Churchward at Swindon, and the GWR '4300' class which first appeared in 1911 was undoubtedly the result of Holcroft's recommendation. Gresley, then, seeking right away to establish his reputation with an advanced design, adopted the 2-6-0 type for a new 5ft 8in mixed traffic locomotive, and took another note of Transatlantic practice by fitting outside cylinders with Walschaerts valve gear to operate piston valves mounted above the cylinders. With a high running plate obviating the need for splashers, but retaining the distinctive double curve of previous Stirling and Ivatt outside cylinder designs, he produced a 20th century locomotive style which met his objectives in a way which perpetuated traditional Great Northern lines yet incorporated up-to-the minute developments.

In the following year, 1913, the same design principles were applied to a 2-8-0 type, which enabled the mineral hauls from New England, Peterborough, to Ferme Park, Hornsey, to be increased from 60 to 80 loose coupled wagons. At the same time it was realised that the original 2-6-0 could be improved by the provision of a larger boiler, of the same diameter as that of the 2-8-0s, and so 1914 saw the introduction of the class to be known in LNER days as the 'K2'.

Despite the intervention of World War 1, a number of development projects were initiated, and in particular, progress was made towards what was to be in later years a Gresley characteristic — 3-cylinder propulsion with the operation of the inside valves derived from the valve gear of the outside cylinders. This led to the emergence in 1918 of a 3-cylinder version of his 2-8-0, but the derived gear fitted to this locomotive was unnecessarily complex, and when in his next design he applied the 3-cylinder technique to his successful 2-6-0 type, he adopted a simplified system based on work by Holcroft.

Concurrently with the construction of new freight and mixed traffic locomotives, quiet but far reaching development was taking place in the passenger engine field. The Great Northern's front line express locomotives at the time were Ivatt's large Atlantics, the last batch emerging from Doncaster in 1910, an advance on the original design through the introduction of superheating, larger cylinders and piston valves. But from his earliest days as Locomotive Engineer of the Great Northern, Gresley had his eyes fixed firmly on a new express passenger engine, one which would place the Great Northern — and himself — firmly in the forefront of exponents of locomotive design. Not, after all, an unworthy ambition for an engineer younger than most of his contemporaries, and who already had two advanced designs to his credit. So, it was in 1922 that he produced his new express locomotive, GNR No 1470, incorporating all that he considered best in contemporary British and US practice — large boiler with wide firebox, three cylinders, and high running plate, all contributing to a well-proportioned Pacific, from which all subsequent LNER 4-6-2 designs were to be developed.

The introduction of the new 'quad-art' sets of articulated coaches for the London suburban traffic called for more powerful tank engines, and Gresley met the need by updating the successful Ivatt 0-6-2T by providing a superheater, piston valves, and larger cylinders, no fewer than 60 being delivered in 1920/21, virtually straight off the drawing board. The only other locomotives built during his period with the Great Northern were for goods traffic. He saw no reason to make major changes to the final Ivatt development of the ubiquitous 5ft 2in 0-6-0 and added 95 to the 15 already built, whilst in another 1913 design he broke away from the GNR tradition of saddle tanks for yard shunting duties by introducing a 0-6-0T with elongated side tanks incorporating tapered front ends to aid visibility and openings at running plate level to provide access to the motion. Otherwise, little was changed from a Stirling design of 1874. These 0-6-0Ts, LNER Class J50, were to be built at intervals almost throughout the lifespan of the LNER and indeed at one time were proposed by Thompson as a postwar standard design.

Following the 1923 grouping and Gresley's appointment as CME of the LNER, one might have expected a wide-ranging survey of the locomotive stock of the new group, and proposals for standardisation. But apart from a comprehensive system of classification, which must have brought home the diversity of locomotive stock the new railway had inherited, no proposals for rationalisation were formulated. Indeed, the new CME was evidently told early on that money would not be available for large scale scrap and replacement, and that whereas the Board would approve an annual building programme, this would necessarily be modest in relation to the locomotive stock of the company

New designs would be introduced as opportunity permitted, although in the early years of the grouping much new construction was to be of appropriate pre-grouping classes. As new locomotives became available, transfers took place between Areas, experimental work continued with the objective of improving efficiency and reliability, and, later, selected classes were the subject of major rebuilding.

Gresley did not believe in building small engines which had to be thrashed to cope with their payloads, and in general his locomotives had something in hand in their day-to-day working, possessing the capability to meet an overload when necessary. This was particularly the case in the late 1930s, when the LNER's 'Big Engine' reputation became established, enabling the railway to cope with extremes of load during the war years and after. At no time did Gresley publish plans for a comprehensive fleet of standard locomotives. In fact, his views on standard locomotives were succinctly expressed when in 1918 the Association of Railway Locomotive Engineers was endeavouring to promote a series of standard locomotives capable of employment on most of the major railways; he stated that he was a strong advocate of standardisation in principle, but not of locomotives.

The situation at the grouping was such that although new engines were needed for certain specific tasks, the position was not desperate overall; indeed, the majority of the locomotive stock was to soldier on for a good many more years. Of the 7,392 steam engines on the books at the grouping, only 1,256 were withdrawn during the first 10 years of the LNER. During the same period, 956 locomotives were built or purchased. However in 1923, two main needs were identified, in the requirements for more powerful passenger locomotives for the East Coast main line, and for strong mixed traffic engines for several parts of the system. Fortunately, appropriate Gresley designs were available, and construction was put in hand of further Pacifics at Doncaster, and, because of the urgency, by the North British Locomotive Company, whilst Darlington was kept busy in 1924/25 turning out 3-cylinder 2-6-0s, LNER Class K3. A bonus was discovered in that large numbers of Robinson's GCR 2-8-0 design were available at low cost from War Department surplus sources, and the purchase of 273 in three batches of these removed the need for the construction of heavy freight locomotives until 1932, although two large 2-8-2s were built in 1925 to demonstrate the feasibility of hauling 100 wagon coal trains on the GN main line.

In the meantime, existing pre-grouping programmes drawn up by the constituent companies were completed, and consideration given to the provision of locomotives for lesser duties. The Scottish Area was most in need, and to permit the withdrawal of older 4-4-0s, new medium power locomotives were needed. Refusing a request for another batch of NB 'Scotts', Gresley selected the Robinson 'Director' class, the strongest of the constituent companies' 4-4-0s, to meet the need until a group standard class could be introduced; this arrived in 1927, in the shape of the 'D49' 'Shire' class. The previous year Darlington had produced the first LNER standard 5ft 2in 0-6-0, the 'J39'. The first 35 in fact were built with 4ft 8in wheels for the Fife coalfield traffic, Class J38.

In a characteristic effort to produce horses for courses, Gresley's reponse to the need for more suburban tanks was threefold. He repeated his own design of 0-6-2T, the 'N2', for Great Northern and North British services, whilst on the Great Eastern, where the main need was for smart acceleration between closely spaced suburban stations, further orders were placed for Hill's 4ft 10in 0-6-2T, Class N7. But for longer distance traffic in the North East, Gresley provided locomotives of another Robinson design, the 'A5' 4-6-2T, the only existing LNER tank class capable of this work apart from the NER 'H1' 4-4-4T which even on its own ground was regarded as only mediocre and which was later rebuilt as the 'A8' 4-6-2T.

Although Robinson did not succeed to the position of CME of the LNER, *his* influence continued to permeate the LNER locomotive stock. If he had kept count, it would have given him great pleasure to discover that up the end of 1929, locomotives built to his designs for the LNER (including the bought-in 2-8-0s) totalled 330; during the same period, 442 were built to Gresley's designs. Although the figure of Robinson's locomotives is heavily biassed by the number of ex-WD engines, the proportion illustrates the regard the Gresley must have had for the older man, as well as forming a tribute to the simple ruggedness of the three designs, the 'D11' 'Directors', the 'A5s', and the '04' 2-8-0s. In these locomotives, Robinson had got his proportions right — something he never seemed to achieve in his 4-6-0s.

Gresley's standard GNR shunting tank, the 'J50' 0-6-0T, continued to be built during his LNER days, supplemented by two batches of heavy shunting tanks. These were, in 1925, five 'T1' 4-8-0T, perpetuating a Wilson Worsdell design of 1909, and in 1932, yet another contribution by Robinson, two 'S1' 0-8-4T. But Gresley's major short distance freight locomotive was the massive 'U1', the 2-8-0+0-8-2 Garratt, built in 1925 virtually as a double '02', for banking the Worsborough incline near Wath. At the other end of the scale, 58 small Sentinel 0-4-0Ts were purchased for lightweight freight and shunting duties, including service in the company's shops. Sentinel also contributed the majority of a series of steam railcars introduced in an effort to provide a low cost solution to branch line operation.

Early experience with the Pacifics showed that the full benefit of the boiler's steaming capability could not be obtained because of inadequate valve design, which had an unnecessarily throttling effect. Experiments with redesigned valve gear and higher boiler pressure resulted in the 'A3' 'Super-Pacific' version, giving better performance on the road, and significantly lower fuel and water consumption.

Concurrently with this investigation into the Pacific design, Gresley was endeavouring to produce a 4-6-0 for the heaviest Great Eastern services, but unfortunately the locomotive he would like to have was unacceptable to the Civil Engineer, and the delay whilst this was under investigation led to emergency measures. In 1928 a further 10 Holden 'B12' 4-6-0s were built by Beyer Peacock, followed shortly afterwards by a new class, the 'B17' 'Sandringhams', designed and built by the North British Locomotive Company, but incorporating much of the design work of Gresley's abortive proposals. The 'Sandringham' class continued to be built until 1937, by which time a further proposal had been made to introduce a 4-6-0, but again this was not proceeded with.

Forced by circumstances to make the best of his ageing fleet of pre-grouping locomotives, and at the same time to seek improvements in components which could contribute in some way to greater efficiency and reduce maintenance, Gresley experimented with alternative types of superheaters, feed water heaters, draughting arrangements, lubrication systems and other ancilliary features. He paid particular attention to valve design, and built or rebuilt a number of locomotives of various classes with different versions of poppet valves. The Great Eastern 'B12s', the 'Claud Hamiltons' and larger 0-6-0s were subjected to rebuilding on Gresley lines, as well as some North Eastern 'B16' mixed traffic 4-6-0s and a few Robinson 2-8-0s. Other North Eastern classes to be looked at were the express passenger 'D20' 4-4-0s and the 'C7' Atlantics, two of which were rebuilt with boosters in 1931. But Gresley's major piece of experimentation was his massive 4-6-4, evocatively numbered 10000, completed at the end of 1929 in association with Yarrow & Co of Glasgow, with a marine type boiler and compound propulsion. Never reliable, it was eventually to be rebuilt on more conventional lines and take its place alongside the later streamlined Pacifics.

The 1930s saw a number of new Gresley designs. Of these, the 'V1' 2-6-2T, was his first to be constructed for outer suburban duties. These were built in batches up to 1940, the last 10, Class V3, having higher boiler pressure. But in 1934 and the two succeeding years the designs which were to be his masterpieces were introduced: the 'P2' 2-8-2 *Cock o' the North,* the streamline Pacifics, truly his chef d'oeuvre, and the 'V2' 2-6-2 mixed traffic locomotives, a class which would have numbered over 200 had a later batch not been cancelled during the war. it was these big engines, and the steamline trains, which caught the public imagination in the final years of peace, placing the LNER, and Nigel Gresley, high in public acclaim.

Gresley's last two steam classes, although similar in certain aspects, were intended for quite different purposes. The first, the 'K4', introduced in 1937, consisted of six powerful 2-6-0s, specifically for the West Highland line. The second, the 'V4', in effect a scaled down 'V2', was to be his all-purpose locomotive, the Gresley equivalent of the Stanier 'Black Five'. At the same time as the 'V4' was introduced, in February 1941, the Press were given a preview of things to come in the shape of the 1,500V dc mixed traffic Bo-Bo No 6701, the prototype of a class designed to work over the electrified Great Central line over the Pennines from Manchester to Sheffield and Wath.

Nigel Gresley died two months before he would have reached the age of 65. For some years he had not been in the best of health; had he lived, would he have retired at 65? In normal circumstances, probably yes, but in wartime he might well have stayed on. If he had done so, Edward Thompson might not have had the opportunity to succeed him, and the Thompson variant of the Gresley theme not have been seen. The LNER Board seem to have taken no steps to have a successor waiting in the wings to follow Gresley, so the conclusion must be that he was expected to remain in office at least for the time being.

If the LNER had not been nationalised, Arthur Peppercorn would probably have succeeded in due course, followed by J. F. Harrison, appointed by Peppercorn as his Assistant, and who, a staunch devotee of Gresley, took a leading part in the final development of the LNER family of Pacifics. But even if there had been no nationalisation, adverse environmental conditions, unwillingness to work in the dirty and uncomfortable surroundings unavoidably associated with steam traction when better paid and more congenial work was available elsewhere, and in particular the arrival of more efficient diesel-electric power, meant inevitably that steam was approaching the end of its useful life as the prime source of railway motive power. Indeed, 15 years after the demise of the LNER, steam had all but disappeared from the East Coast scene.

There was no delay however in replacing Gresley, nor does there appear to have been any competition for his post. Sir Ronald Matthews canvassed views on the desirability of contacting Bulleid, in case he could be attracted back into the Company in which he had spent so much of his working life, but it was concluded that he would prefer to remain on the Southern and see his newly introduced 'Merchant Navy' class into successful service. Another possible candidate was R. C. Bond of the LMS, but it was thought unlikely that Stanier would let him go.

And so, in the event, the choice fell on Edward Thompson, the most senior of the LNER's mechanical engineers, currently at Doncaster as Mechanical Engineer, Southern Area, (Western Section). At a Board meeting on 24 April 1941, after recording with profound regret the great loss the Company had sustained in the death of Sir Nigel and paying particular tribute to his professional ability and skill, the Board went on to appoint Thompson as CME, although with somewhat reduced powers. To his chagrin, the Electrical Engineering Department was hived off as a separate entity under H. W. H Richards, whilst the CME's privilege of accepting pupils was withdrawn. However Thompson managed to maintain his personal location at Doncaster, moving the CME's office there from Kings Cross, at the same time arranging a redistribution of duties within his Department, resulting in the redeployment of Gresley's closest associates.

Much has been made of the reportedly strained relationship between Thompson and Gresley, even to the extent that Thompson possessed an intense dislike for his Chief. Possibly the Thompson syndrome sprang from the personality of the man himself. Excessively fastidious about his personal appearance, possessed of an unpredictable temper, never a person to mix easily with his subordinates, in many ways he was the antithesis of Gresley. He joined the North Eastern Railway in 1906, transferring to the Great Northern in 1912 when, under Gresley, he took over his Chief's old post as Carriage and Wagon Superintendent. In 1913 Thompson married Raven's younger daughter, and no doubt continued to be imbued with Darlington thinking. He returned to the North Eastern in 1920 as Carriage and Wagon Works Manager at York, but Gresley brought him back into the locomotive arena when he became Assistant Mechanical Engineer at Stratford in 1927, to be Mechanical Engineer there three years later. He was later further promoted to similar positions at Darlington and Doncaster, and Gresley must have appreciated Thompson's ability by these successive promotions, despite the obvious fact that he was 'difficult to manage'. Possibly as the 1930s wore on, they drifted apart, Thompson being away from the mainstream of locomotive policy, whilst Gresley confided in those closer to him, Bulleid and Spencer. Unfortunately, Gresley is known to have corrected Thompson in front of subordinates, a mistaken tactic anyway, but unforgivable in Thompson's eyes.

Although Thompson prided himself on his ability as an engineer, he was primarily an engineering manager. He saw clearly the advantages to be derived from a programme of locomotive standardisation with fewer differing classes needing a smaller range of parts to maintain them. He realised too the benefits which would accrue from simpler design, and, in particular, in the short term, from a reorganisation of arrangements for locomotive repairs. Probably he was impatient with Gresley's policy of building comparatively expensive machines for specific duties, such as the 'K4', and indeed the 'O2', regarded as the Rolls Royce of freight engines. In particular he could not comprehend the reasoning behind the complexity of the maid-of-all-work 'V4', a class which was needed in quantity.

Although Thompson has been quoted as telling his senior staff that he had much to do, and little time in which to do it, the circumstances of the war years undoubtedly prevented him from doing as much as otherwise might have been possible. Nevertheless he laid the foundations of the LNER postwar locomotive building programme, which enlarged the fleet by almost a thousand new engines. His reputation however foundered in the eyes of many railwaymen and

26

enthusiasts when he destroyed two of Gresley's most cherished locomotives, *Cock o' the North* and *Great Northern*, in his single minded efforts to produce successors to the Gresley designs which he hoped would prove easier to maintain.

He started slowly enough, and his first programme, approved in September 1941, comprised 65 locomotives of three Gresley classes — 30 'V2', 20 'V3' and 15 'J50'. However the drawing office was at work on alternatives even whilst these proposals were being formulated, and in the event none of these 65 were built. In March 1942 a decision was taken to cancel all outstanding 'J50s' and in their place to substitute plans to rebuild a like number of old Great Central 0-8-0s of Class Q4, by shortening their boilers and adding side tanks, releasing their tenders for use on other locomotives. In December 1942 the first of his mixed traffic 4-6-0s appeared, in the form of No 8301 *Springbok*, receiving commendation from all sides, but his next move, the rebuilding of 'P2' No 2005 *Thane of Fife* led to the consequences for which he has been so strongly criticised; when the engine reappeared as a Pacific it was totally unrecognisable as the locomotive it has been a few months before. The remaining 'P2s' were also dealt with in this way, and the last four 'V2s' to be built at Darlington were stretched into similar Pacific form. These provided the basis of Thompson's subsequent design of 6ft 2in Pacific, whilst equivalent treatment of *Great Northern* produced a 6ft 8in prototype, the principal non-Gresley features of both being the positioning of the outside cylinders behind the bogie, divided drive to the coupled wheels, and inclusion of a third set of Walschaerts valve gear in place of the derived motion.

In pursuit of his objective of simplifying the Gresley designs, and producing prototypes for his standardisation programme, Thompson rebuilt a number of other locomotives, some of which formed the basis of classes which were later built or rebuilt in quantity. Most of these conversions were to form part of his formal programme of standardisation, promulgated in April 1945, in which he postulated 10 standard locomotive types. These included an 'A1' Pacific, with 6ft 8in wheels, and a similar 'A2' with coupled wheels 6in smaller, although the justification for two classes so alike in almost every other dimension is difficult to discern. Then there were the long awaited 6ft 2in 4-6-0, the 'B1', and the 'K1', a 2-cylinder rebuild of Gresley's 5ft 2in 'K4', (or, as was expressed in the programme, 'an engine of similar power'; one wonders what the alternative might have been). A rebuild of yet another Robinson design, the 'J11' 0-6-0, would deal with lighter freight traffic, the Robinson 'O4' rebuilt as the 'O1' would be the heavy mineral locomotive, whilst the freight tank engines would be the 'Q1' rebuild of the 'Q4', the 'J50' (the only Gresley design selected unaltered), and a light shunting engine, as then undecided. Thompson's large passenger tank, the 'L1' 2-6-4T completed the list, but this was generally regarded as a failure; too powerful for its structure, it ran ragged very quickly.

Concurrently with the publication of the list of standard locomotives, the LNER announced that it was proposed to maintain the existing fleet of Pacifics and 'V2s', 'V1s' rebuilt as 'V3s', 'B16s' rebuilt with three sets of valve gear, 'B17s' and 'K3s' rebuilt with two outside cylinders, and 'D49s' rebuilt with two inside cylinders. Two provisos were written into the package, to the effect that the numbers and types of locomotives to be built or rebuilt were to be reviewed in the light of their performance in traffic, whilst it was also acknowledged that the development of diesel power might affect the future building of steam engines.

Whilst these proposals were being finalised, nationalisation was less than three years away, and Thompson had little more than another year in office, but he received approval in principle for a five year programme under which 1,000 locomotives were to be withdrawn and replaced by new construction. He was succeeded on 1 July 1946 by Arthur Peppercorn, a likeable character who, with the willing support of his staff, set about rectifying the main defects of the Thompson Pacifics, whilst raising the momentum of the postwar building plans. Altogether a further 79 Pacifics were built, another 400 'B1s' to add to the original 10, 70 'K1s', 100 'L1s', and, as light shunting tanks, 28 'J72' 0-6-0Ts, of an 1898 Wilson Worsdell design. 200 'Austerity' 2-8-0s and 75 0-6-0STs were purchased from Government disposal agencies, whilst under BR interest switched from 'J50s' to 350hp diesel-electrics. So, in the main, the Thompson postwar building plan was implemented, but it was quietly decided that no massive rebuilding would take place, and Gresley's three-cylinder engines continued, with very few exceptions, in their original form, derived gear notwithstanding. In fact, construction of tender engines to LNER design continued until the last 'B1', No 61399, was delivered from the North British Locomotive Company in April 1952, by which time the introduction of BR standard locomotives was well under way. So it may be said that No 61399 was the last of the line, the final locomotive to be built in the LNER tradition, with the influence of Nigel Gresley still coming through strongly.

Two later schools of design also owe something to Gresley: Oliver Bulleid's Pacifics for the Southern Railway, and certain aspects of the BR standard locomotives, culminating in the *Duke of Gloucester*. Indeed, in the long and fascinating story of the steam locomotive, it is a fitting tribute to the influence of Sir Nigel Gresley that this last British express engine should follow his principles of large boiler, wide firebox, and 3-cylinder propulsion.

Chapter 3

The Big Engines

During the latter part of this period of office, Henry Ivatt had provided the Great Northern with a fleet of 94 large boilered Atlantics, which coped adequately with the needs of the express services of the period. The final batch of 10, produced in 1910, were built with piston valves and Schmidt superheaters, and demonstrated improved performance at greater efficiency, although in accordance with conventional thought at the time, steam pressure was reduced from 175 to 150lb/sq in. Two years later, Nigel Gresley, now responsible for the locomotive stock, lost no time in making detail improvements to selected engines in line with contemporary practice, and to further his own ideas on locomotive design. Nevertheless, by 1918 the increasing East Coast loads of the period indicated that even the Atlantics had their limitations. Trains out of Kings Cross were regularly loading to over 450 tons, well over the weight the Atlantics were designed to lift up to Potters Bar, so, whilst generally maintaining point-to-point timings, piloting was necessary over this initial stretch of line. Wartime conditions no doubt delayed the introduction of a successor to the Atlantics, but Gresley had been quietly working on this for several years. He visualised a big multi-cylindered design, to be as much in advance as its contemporaries as the Atlantics had been in their day.

The success of the superheated Atlantics led Gresley to decide at an early stage that if he was to provide a boiler large enough to generate all the steam he would need, and a wide firebox to enable the fireman to keep a large fire going for a long period, a 2-6-2 or 4-6-2 type would be called for. His initial considerations included a 2-6-2 incorporating the pony truck already successfully employed on his 2-6-0s, which had the capability for fairly high speed running, but this was discarded in favour of a Pacific. To obtain experience of multi-cylinder operation, as early as 1913 designs were prepared for an experimental rebuilding of Atlantic No 279 with four 15in×26in cylinders and outside Walschaerts valve gear operating the inside piston valves by means of rocking shafts. The rebuild entered traffic in 1915, and about the same time Doncaster produced an outline of a 4-cylinder Pacific which owed a great deal to the Ivatt Atlantic profile. However in 1916 Gresley's attention was drawn to the publication in 'Engineering' of detailed drawings of a carefully developed 4-6-2 built by the Pennsylvania Railroad in May 1914 as the first of a class, huge by British standards, known as the 'K4s' (the suffix denoting that the engines were superheated) and eventually to

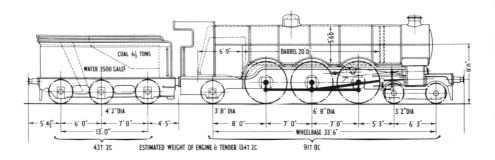

COAL 6¼ TONS

WATER 3500 GALLS

6' 9"

BARREL 20' 0"

5' 6"

6' 0"

4' 2" DIA

3' 8" DIA

6' 8" DIA

3' 2" DIA

5' 4¼"   6' 0"   7' 0"   4' 5"   8' 0"   7' 0"   7' 0"   5' 3"   6' 3"

13' 0"   WHEELBASE 33' 6"

43T. 2C   ESTIMATED WEIGHT OF ENGINE & TENDER 134T. 2C   91T. 0C

Early outline of 4-cylinder Pacific of 1915

reach a total of 425 by 1928. Tests of the prototype at the Altoona test plant proved it to be a well-proportioned design, with a 19ft taper boiler possessing a total heating surface of 5,189sq ft, more than adequate to raise steam for the two 27in×28in cylinders; boiler pressure was 205lb/sq in. The Belpaire firebox had a wide grate with an area of 69.5sq ft, which must have called for superhuman firing in the days before mechanical stokers were introduced. Gresley was reported to have been very impressed with the proportions of the 'K4s', but even when scaled down not all aspects of the design were wholly relevant to the Great Northern. True, Ivatt had already used the wide firebox, whilst Churchward favoured the taper boiler, and Gresley adopted these features, but not the Belpaire firebox. He also took note of certain details, such as the 3-bar pattern of slidebar. One particular attribute however could not be built into any British design. In common with American practice in placing as much as possible of the machinery outside the frames, the 'K4s' had two large outside cylinders, but GNR platform clearances could not tolerate a diameter even approaching 27in, so this aspect of American design was not to be followed; instead, Gresley became convinced of the advantages, as he saw them, of 3-cylinder propulsion. Evidently satisfied with the prospect of correct operation of his derived valve gear, and not wanting to incur the expense of a fourth cylinder and its associated complication in the manufacture of the driving axle, he settled on the 3-cylinder configuration which was to remain one of his major design characteristics throughout the remainder of his career. He argued that the more even turning moment would enable a loco- motive to run better with less wear to its machinery and tyres, and by reducing the hammer blow inherent in reciprocating motion, wear on the track would also be reduced. He also expounded two further principles: that all three cylinders should drive on to the same axle, and that this should not be the leading coupled axle. However, these principles could not always be kept.

By 1920 the need for the new Pacific was becoming urgent, but in the meantime Gresley had given priority to the development of 3-cylinder propulsion in the 10 large 2-6-0s of 1920/21, so it was not until April 1922 that No 1470, first of the long awaited Gresley Pacifics emerged from Doncaster. Named *Great Northern* before it left the works, it made an immediate impression on the contemporary engineering scene, and clearly established Nigel Gresley, and the railway whose name it bore, in the forefront of practitioners of advanced locomotive design. Whilst the majority of pre-grouping railways possessed 4-6-0s of varying capability, only the Great Western had produced a Pacific, and this, *The Great Bear*, dating from 1908, was basically a stretched 'Star', whose appearance and performance by no means matched up to the promise of its increased dimensions. Mechanically and visually, *Great Northern* was composed as an entity, not as an enlargement of a previous design, but as a harmonious whole. The design had evolved gradually as component details were added or modified, and when completed formed a synthesis of all which in Gresley's estimation contributed to the best in contemporary steam locomotive practice. The result turned out to be the most elegant large steam passenger locomotive ever built.

Great Northern and its stable companion *Sir Frederick Banbury*, completed in July 1922, and named after the last Chairman of the Great Northern Railway, both soon to disappear from the railway scene, were at first treated with the circumspection to which they were entitled. Railwaymen had to come to terms with the unprecedented length of the engines, and their girth. But early problems seem to have been of a minor nature, and after gently running up to Kings Cross for inspection, leaving unforgettable impressions on lineside observers, the two Pacifics were soon working heavy expresses between London and Doncaster. Gresley's traffic objective for the class in fact was to haul 600 tons in the schedules of the day, with average speeds around 50mph, and this they proved well capable of doing.

Dimensionally the Pacifics were well proportioned, the boiler having 3,455sq ft of heating surface, with a firebox of 41.25sq ft grate area, and three 20in×26in cylinders. Boiler pressure at 180lb/sq in broke no new ground, but Gresley at that time adhered to the belief that there was no merit in higher boiler pressure as such, whilst construction and maintenance costs would be increased unnecessarily. Tractive effort was 29,835lb. With proper firing, little difficulty was reported in providing the cylinders with adequate steam from the tapered boiler, 6ft 5in at its maximum diameter. There was however a design weakness in that the valve movements tended to restrict steam flow unnecessarily. Piston valves of 8in diameter were fitted, but following experience with the derived gear on the 3-cylinder 2-6-0s, in which the centre valve tended to overtravel at high speeds, the maximum valve travel was reduced in the Pacifics. This remedy was not to prove successful, adversely affecting starting and acceleration, as well as causing higher fuel and water consumption. However later redesign of the valve gear was to result in significant improvement.

After the grouping, with Gresley firmly in the CME's saddle, it was inconceivable that any design of Pacific other than his own would be adopted for all-line service. But as the North Eastern, in a final gesture of independence, had produced the Darlington version of this type, trials were arranged between the two classes. The Raven Pacific would have had to be outstandingly the better of the two to triumph over its Great Northern rival, and this was not to be the case; in the summer of 1923 comparative running between examples of each class showed little difference in performance, the Doncaster design returning a slightly lower fuel consumption. Whilst still independent the GNR Board had sanctioned a further 10 Gresley Pacifics (LNER Nos 4472-81) and the first of these, constructed at Doncaster, was in traffic by February 1923. Three further Raven 4-6-2s emerged from Darlington in March 1924, but by that time the decision had been taken by the LNER Board to place orders for a further 40 to the Gresley design. Twenty of these (Nos 2543-62) came from Doncaster for Great Northern sheds, whilst of the balance, (Nos 2563-82) built by the North British Locomotive Company, five went to Haymarket, Edinburgh, 10 went to Gateshead, and the final five to Heaton. The Scottish drivers took to them at once, as bigger and better than anything they had seen before, but those based at Tyneside sheds did not at first receive a welcome. In fact, in efforts to resolve the antagonism of the North Eastern enginemen, Gresley himself attended a meeting held to allow the drivers to express themselves about their new engines. However matters settled down before long, particularly as shortcomings became evident on the Raven Pacifics, which developed a propensity to run hot. Clearly this class did not possess the potential of the Gresley variety, but the Raven Pacifics were not entirely ignored, and in 1929 one was fitted with a Gresley boiler, firebox and cab, and later the original six-wheeled tenders of the class were replaced by eight-wheel tenders of LNER pattern. However the class, small in number, were expensive to maintain in service, and understandably all five were withdrawn in 1936/7.

The LNER were rightly proud of their new Pacifics, and in 1924 arranged for the first post-grouping example, No 4472 *Flying Scotsman*, to appear as an exhibit in the Palace of Engineering at the British Empire Exhibition at Wembley. On a closely adjoining stand was the newly completed GWR 4-6-0, No 4073 *Caerphilly Castle*. Noticeably smaller, and of an earlier, Edwardian, appearance, the 'Castle' was proclaimed as the most powerful locomotive in Britain. How could this be, asked the unenlightened, when the Pacific was so obviously bigger? The matter was destined to be settled by trial, when in 1925 exchanges were arranged under which the LNER Pacific was to run on the Great Western in comparative tests with a native 'Castle', whilst Pacific and 'Castle' would be similarly pitted against one another on the LNER. To the dismay of many LNER staff and enthusiasts, not only did the 'Castles' prove superior to the Pacifics, but the Great Western stage managed their part of the affair better, deriving a maximum of favourable publicity. It is fair to say that the Pacific was not the most suitable type for the sinuous and undulating GWR line between Reading and Plymouth, but oddly this was where the Gresley design began to show its merits as the week of the trials progressed. But on the Great Northern main line, the 'Castle', casually ignoring speed restrictions, and in competition with Pacifics not in the best condition or handled as competently as they might have been, consistently turned in superior performances. Astonishingly, Gresley was not consulted at the time the trials were initiated, and these were said to have been the outcome of a social conversation between Sir Felix Pole, the GWR General Manager, and Alex Wilson, the LNER Southern Area Divisional General Manager. In a somewhat lame apologia to his Directors, Gresley asserted that the trials had not really provided a fair comparison, as the capabilities of his engines had not been fully exploited.

The prime reason for the superiority of the 'Castles' is clear, and should have been seen at the time: The Pacific's valve design was too restrictive to take full advantage of the steaming capability of the boiler. Spencer had earlier pointed this out to Gresley, and in 1924 had produced a redesign incorporating longer valve travel and longer lap, although retaining the original 8in diameter valves. But the CME was understandably reluctant to alter a design still comparatively new, and which — although with some concern over higher than expected fuel consumption — was master of the tasks it was set. Even after the message had been clearly spelled out, in the performance of the 'Castles', Gresley was slow to move. Not until May 1927, following a series of experiments, were instructions issued to convert the Pacifics to a modified design of valve gear, incorporating the lessons learned in the past few years. The results were far-reaching, the immediate payback being a reduction in coal consumption such that non-stop running between Kings Cross and Edinburgh Waverley became a practicability. The introduction of corridor tenders enabled crews to be changed en route, and this longest non-stop schedule in railway history commenced operating in the summer timetable of 1928, although due to a long standing (and restrictive) agreement with the operators of the West Coast route from Euston the 392.7 miles continued to be spun out over $8\frac{1}{4}$ hours, at an overall speed of barely $47\frac{1}{2}$mph. The next development followed the adoption of another feature of the 'Castles', and was a 22% increase in boiler pressure, to 220lb/sq in. This too was introduced in 1927, and in the following two years 10 additions (Nos 2743-52) made to the stud of Pacifics were to the new specification, as Class A3, with long travel valves, higher boiler pressure, and 19in×26in cylinders, tractive effort being 32,909lb. Eventually all the original 'A1s' (later classed 'A10') were converted to 'A3s', but whereas all had had their valve gear altered by 1931, apart from five which received 220lb boilers in 1927/8 no more boiler upgradings took place until the war years, in order to obtain the maximum life from the original boilers. The 'A3' could be easily distinguished from the 'A1' by the cover plates on each side of the upper part of the smokebox, which were necessitated by the wider header of the 43-element superheater with which these locomotives were fitted. Eight more 'A3s' (Nos 2595-99 and 2795-97) were constructed in 1930, but the final batch (Nos 2500-08) did not enter service until 1934/5. These last examples featured a new device in the form of a steam collector integral with the dome, intended to separate out particles of water and so ensure maximum dryness of steam entering the cylinders.

Whilst the basic design of Pacific was being refined by successive developments, Gresley had been directing his inventiveness to the fundamental problem of generating steam more effectively, and had applied a high pressure marine type water tube boiler to a Pacific type wheelbase, in the event elongated to a 4-6-4 type, Class W1, which entered traffic at the beginning of 1930. This example of practical research was produced in conjunction with Harold Yarrow of the Glasgow firm of marine engineers which had provided the boiler, whilst the locomotive was erected in conditions of great secrecy at Darlington. Of unconventional appearance, the engine was dubbed the 'Hush-hush', a soubriquet enhanced by the dark grey livery of the engine, and its number, 10000. Indeed, knowledge of its existence was denied to the LNER Board, at least so far as the official record goes. It was never included in a formal building programme, and presumably was justified on the basis of its experimental potential; possibly it was partly financed by Yarrow, foreseeing market possibilities if this adaption of their product turned out to be successful. However this was not to be the case, although the locomotive demonstrated its capabilities on occasion by working important

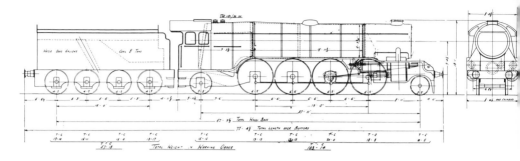

Early outline of 'P2', April 1933. Note the plain lines. *Crown Copyright, National Railway Museum, York*

trains such as the non-stop 'Flying Scotsman'. Steaming was uncertain, and the boiler was prone to tube leakage, confirming what was undoubtedly foreseen, that there would be difficulties in applying a marine type of technology to the confined space and continuous flexing of a locomotive. In 1937 No 10000 was reconstructed as a 3-cylinder simple locomotive on the lines of the contemporary streamlined 'A4s', and as such, with 20in×26in cylinders and 250lb/sq in boiler pressure, it was the most powerful 6ft 8in locomotive ever built in Britain. However as is so often the case with one-offs, it never seemed to realise its full potential in service nor did it appear to figure in any of Gresley's later ideas for development. But its designer's courage in bringing the original unconventional design to revenue earning service was another example of the work which earned him the respect of his professional colleagues.

The depression years of the early 1930s brought no overt signs of new developments in the LNER locomotive scene, but important work was taking place in the design offices. This was initially concerned with the evolution of a more powerful engine to work the overnight sleeping-car trains over the difficult road between Edinburgh and Aberdeen, made considerably heavier by the introduction in 1928 of sleeping-car facilities for third class passengers, and for which double heading was necessary, even with Pacifics. This challenge from the Operating Department was one which Gresley relished, and resulted in the renowned 'P2s', of the 2-8-2 'Mikado' type, the most powerful passenger locomotive class to be built for service in Britain before steam gave way to other forms of motive power. The first, No 2001, appropriately named *Cock o' the North*, featured a 50sq ft firegrate, and with a 220lb/sq in boiler, 21in×26in cylinders and 6ft 2in coupled wheels, tractive effort was 43,462lb. Heating surface was 3,490sq ft. No 2001 incorporated several concepts new to British express locomotive practice. These included the unique eight coupled wheelbase, Lentz poppet valves operated by rotary cams (already tried on smaller engines), smokebox sidesheets derived from those on No 10000, and, as imports from France, a wedge shaped spectacle plate and steam passages and draughting based on principles expounded by M. André Chapelon of the Chemin-de-Fer Paris-Orleans. *Cock o' the North* was sent to the French locomotive testing station at Vitry-sur-Seine, and whilst showing up well on power and output efficiency tests, certain design shortcomings were exposed. In practice, the cams operating the

34

poppet valves proved unsatisfactory, and the second 'P2', No 2002 *Earl Marischal,* was turned out with conventional 9in piston valves and derived gear to operate the inside valves. However steam was not exhausted by the piston valves as sharply as by the poppet valves, and drifting smoke and steam became a serious problem. This was partially alleviated by provision of a second set of side screens, fitted outside the originals, but which tended to restrict forward visibility from the cab. Later, when the wedge shaped outline of the 'A4s' had proved successful as an aid to smoke lifting, four more 'P2s' (Nos 2003-2006) were turned out with this profile, whilst Nos 2001 and 2002 were altered to conform, No 2001 being converted to piston valve operation at the same time.

The 'P2s' were truly a masterpiece of the locomotive builder's art: but the question may be asked, were they really necessary? By no means all the trains on the Aberdeen road loaded to over 500 tons; the day trains grossed considerably less, and were well within the capability of the Pacifics. As it was, the 'P2s' spent much of their time waiting at turnround points, or hauling trains which were to them lightweight. Drivers reported that they could walk away with anything which was presented to them, but firemen would become exhausted by the time the halfway stage was reached at Dundee. Moreover, despite the 9ton capacity of their tenders, Scottish coal was of relatively low calorific value and this, combined with the rate of firing, often resulted in the engines arriving at Waverley with their tenders virtually empty. Stories that in the teeth of a south-westerly gale *Cock o' the North* in its original condition had been known to run out of coal by Inverkeithing and had to appropriate the signalman's stock of coal (and even on one occasion the wooden steps of the signalbox) are undoubtedly exaggerated. It is true however that on a test run in the early days, coal had to be taken on at Dalmeny. Alarming statements that the engines were prone to spread the track were also wide of the mark, but undoubtedly the 19ft 6in coupled wheelbase caused occasional derailments in tight corners of locomotive yards. The pattern eventually settled down to one of changing engines at Dundee, so that point-to-point runs were no more than 71 miles (to Aberdeen) or 59 miles (to Edinburgh).

The pattern of employment of the 'P2s' illustrates the power of Gresley's instructions. The class could with advantage have been employed elsewhere particularly later in their career on the heaviest trains on the East Coast route in England, which under wartime conditions were loading to 20 coaches or more. But 'Mr Gresley had said that they were only to be used on the Aberdeen trains', and that was that. True, they did go to Perth, making light of Glenfarg bank, but never on the Waverley route, so far as is known, the locomotives for which were mainly provided by St Margaret's or Carlisle Canal, not Haymarket, which was the Edinburgh home of the 'P2s'. Nevertheless, in the early war years, they did go to Newcastle, but on night trains, so that there was less likelihood of them being seen. On such turns they replaced a combination of a Pacific and a 'D1' 4-4-0.

By 1934, with Britain beginning to climb out of depression, a new commercial impetus was in the air; no longer was the emphasis on hauling heavier trains at moderate speeds, but on higher speed inter-city transits. Whilst Gresley's Pacifics certainly were not sluggards, by contemporary standards, their designer's objective had always appeared as the haulage of heavy trains whilst maintaining scheduled timings. Since *City of Truro's* proclaimed 102mph in 1904, no serious attempt had been made at high speed running, but reports were now coming in from Germany that a two-coach articulated diesel unit, styled the 'Flying Hamburger' was maintaining a speed of 77.4mph over 178 miles, reaching 100mph in the process. The LNER management considered whether they should emulate this, and if so would this mean importation of diesel technology, or could steam do the job as well — or even better? The answer was provided on 30 November 1934 when No 4472 *Flying Scotsman* and four coaches reached Leeds, 185 miles from London, in just under 152 minutes, averaging 73mph. On the return journey, given its head down Stoke Bank, No 4472 just touched 100mph. This satisfied the LNER that Gresley Pacifics could cope equally well with lightweight high-speed trains as with their traditional heavier, but slower, hauls. Nevertheless, the LNER would not provide Spartan accommodation, serving only a cold buffet as the Germans did, but would provide full restaurant facilities. So, in a further proving run, an 'A3', No 2750 *Papyrus*, was put to running a seven coach train to Newcastle in a timing of four hours, which was completed three minutes under schedule despite a severe delay en route from a derailed freight train. *Papyrus* and its train returned to Kings Cross having cut eight minutes from the four hour schedule, including averaging 100mph over a distance of 12 miles, and reaching a top speed of 108mph. True, these figures were achieved on falling gradients, but the feasibility of high speed travel had been demonstrated, and the Great Western and *City of Truro* had been firmly shouldered into second place.

No time was lost in planning the first public high-speed service, which was introduced in September 1935 between Kings Cross and Newcastle, proudly bearing the title 'Silver Jubilee' in commemoration of the Jubilee Year of King George V and Queen Mary. The Chief General Manager, Sir Ralph Wedgwood, is credited with the initiative for introducing the streamline trains, and he was fully backed by Nigel Gresley, who saw further benefits arising from the application of a streamlined outline to his Pacific design, and the provision of a set of streamlined coaches to match, both appropriately finished in silver grey. Together they formed a superb composition which put the LNER in a leading place in contemporary industrial design. Important dimensional changes in the new 'A4' Pacifics built to work the high speed services included a boiler shortened by a foot, compensated for by a corresponding enlargement of the combustion chamber, and an increase in pressure to 250lb/sq in; cylinders were $18\frac{1}{2}$in × 26in and the tractive effort 35,455lb. The diameter of the valves was increased to 9in and attention was paid to smoothing the internal steam passages, to ease the flow of steam into and away from the cylinders.

Authority in the 1934 programme to build four more 'A3s' was interpreted as sanction for the 'A4s', and such was the energy put into the task that less than six months elapsed between commencement of the design work and the emergence of No 2509 *Silver Link* from Doncaster, followed by Nos 2510-12. The 'Silver Jubilee' was introduced to the Press on 27 September 1935, when the high speed propensity of the 'A4s' was demonstrated for the first time: a top speed of 112.5mph was recorded, whilst 100mph was maintained for 43 miles. Nevertheless, in normal service very high speed was the exception; due primarily to the 'A4s' ability to run fast uphill, the four hour schedule between Kings Cross and Newcastle with one stop in each direction could be maintained without difficulty with a maximum speed of no more than 90mph. For the first three weeks of the new service, *Silver Link* operated the train exclusively without suffering any failure in running, despite the need initially to rebuild the brick arch after each daily round trip, due to a fault in its foundations which fortunately corrected itself after a few days. However it must be acknowledged that the train was run in virtually ideal conditions for the locomotive, which was generally working well within itself. Strenuous efforts were made at operating level to keep the road clear, often to the detriment of lesser services, but undoubtedly the prestige induced by the streamline trains set the LNER high in the estimation of the travelling public, and provided the staff with a welcome morale booster.

The success of the 'Silver Jubilee' and the 'A4' class of Pacifics was such that further streamline trains were introduced, the 'Coronation' with one stop in each direction between Kings Cross and Edinburgh, in July 1937, and the 'West Riding Limited', between Kings Cross, Leeds and Bradford, in September 1937. The original four 'A4s' of 1935 were followed by a series of 31, (Nos 4482-4500, 4462-69, 4900-03), representing the entire output of new locomotives from Doncaster Works between December 1936 and July 1938. The first six, painted in LNER green, were named after species of wild birds, and these were followed by a group of five bearing the names of self-governing countries of the British Empire, specifically to work the 'Coronation'. These introduced another new colour scheme, garter blue with dark red wheels, to match the two-tone blue of the 'Coronation' coaches; this blue livery was applied before long to the entire class. Apart from attempts at improvement to the centre big end, the only mechanical change of note during the whole existence of the class was the introduction of Kylchap double blastpipes and chimneys, first applied to No 4468 *Mallard* when it was built in March 1938. The ability to get rid of exhaust steam quickly was a cardinal reason for *Mallard's* achievement on 3 July 1938, when in the course of what was described as 'brake trials' it ran hard down Stoke bank to reach 125mph, suffering no more damage than loss of white metal from the centre big end bearing. Following the success of the double blast pipe and chimney on *Mallard*, the last three 'A4s' were fitted with these improvements from new; eventually all the class were so fitted, but not, strangely enough, until 1957/8.

The mid-1930s were a period of high achievement in the LNER locomotive field, and a further class which was to form an important part of the fleet of big engines was the mixed traffic 'V2' 2-6-2, which was under consideration at the same time as the 'P2s' were being developed. The 'V2s' were intended to work the heavier fast goods services, taking over from the 'K3s', and to replace the various classes of Atlantics, many of which were becoming elderly, on less important passenger trains. In the event the 'V2' proved to be a most successful all-purpose machine, often working in the same rosters as the 'A3s', and on occasion even substituting for a failed 'A4' on a streamline service. At the same time, the class could handle all descriptions of freight working. The design was derived from the 'A3', with a taper boiler 2ft shorter, and three $18\frac{1}{2}$in×26in cylinders contained in a monobloc steel casting which also incorporated the smokebox saddle, steam pipes and steam chests. The grate area was the same as the 'A3', $41\frac{1}{4}$sq ft, and with the 6ft 2in wheel diameter of the 'P2s', tractive effort worked out at 33,370lb, slightly higher than that of the 'A3s'. With the wedge shaped spectacle plate and banjo steam collector, but distinguished from the Pacifics by the absence of splashers, the 'V2s' incorporated the latest detail improvements in design, and the impact of

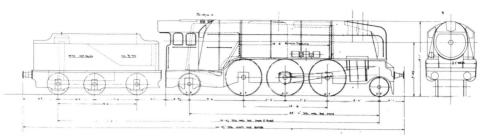

Early outline of 'V2', August 1934. Note rotary cam poppet valve gear, ACFI feedwater heater, Kylchap blast pipe and double chimney. *Crown Copyright, National Railway Museum, York*

their appearance was heightened by painting in passenger green livery. The high axle loading of the class restricted them to the same routes as the Pacifics, which fortunately included the Great Central main line and the Waverley route between Edinburgh and Carlisle, but precluded them from the Great Eastern system and several important subsidiary lines. Although some reservations were expressed at the time of their introduction as to the wisdom of operating fast express trains by locomotives possessing a two wheel leading truck instead of the conventional four wheel bogie, no derailments at speed were reported until 1946, when deteriorating track conditions led to two accidents. As a result, the pony truck was redesigned with side control by springs instead of the previous arrangements with swing links.

The 'V2s' were of immense value to the LNER during the war, and 184 of the class, Nos 4771-4899, 3641-3695, were built between 1936 and 1944, almost all at Darlington, except for the first five and two later batches of 10, which came from Doncaster. The first was named *Green Arrow*, the title given to a new fast goods service introduced by the LNER, and of the others, five commemorated infantry regiments, one receiving its name in BR days, and two were named after public schools in the North Eastern Area. Apart from the change in pony truck design, little was altered during the lifetime of the class. Later on, as cylinders required renewal, the monobloc casting was replaced on a small number of the class by individual components, with prominent outside steampipes. Eight — almost at the end of their days — received double blastpipes and chimneys. An interesting aspect of the design of the 'P2s' and 'V2s' is that the original outline of both was on the lines of the 'A3s', without streamlining or smoke deflectors, and with conventional Walschaerts valve gear. As the designs developed, however,

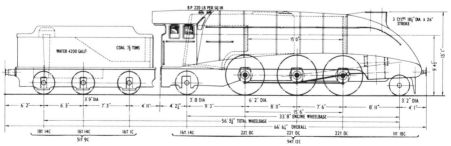

Streamline outline of 'V2', August 1934. *Crown Copyright, National Railway Museum, York*

Lentz valves and boiler casing on the lines of No 10000 were applied to the 'P2', and drawings were made of similar treatment being considered for the 'V2'. Outlines were later produced for each class with streamlined cladding as on the 'A4s', and the 'P2' design with smoke deflecting plates was finally discarded in favour of the wedge shaped front of the 'A4', but the 'V2' emerged unmistakably as a shortened 'A3'.

Maintaining the momentum engendered by the exciting developments of the mid-1930s, Gresley began to look beyond the 'A3s' and 'A4s' to the next generation of his express locomotives, to haul the East Coast trains of the following decade. Two of these proposals were first made known to the outside world when Spencer presented his 1947 Paper to the Institution of Locomotive Engineers, but these never reached the stage of detailed design in the Doncaster drawing office. One was for an improved 'A4', tentatively classed the 'A9', with 275lb/sq in boiler pressure; the other was for an elongated 'A3' in the shape of a 4-8-2 with 21in×26in cylinders, a 250lb/sq in boiler, and a 50sq ft grate. Tractive effort of 45,684lb would have brought the locomotive well into prominence internationally, but with limited information available, several important questions are posed. For example, how would the middle cylinder and its valve gear have been arranged, and what would have been the valve dimensions? The firebox appeared to protrude almost 3ft into the cab, rendering this almost uninhabitable, whilst for how long could a single fireman maintain the firing rate needed for that massive boiler? The proposed 4-8-2 would surely have required mechanical firing to attain its full potential. Gresley had in fact experimented briefly with a mechanical stoker in 1939, but this was on a yard shunter, intended to achieve one man operation, but if the process had been proved, he might have extended the trial to larger locomotives. A painting by Jack Hill of one of these 4-8-2s, purporting to be named *The Great Eastern* gives the impression that it would have been a somewhat ungainly machine. No record has been traced of any proposal to integrate the rebuilt 'W1' 4-6-4 into these advanced plans; perhaps Gresley, unhappy over its lack of success in its original form, had lost interest in the engine.

The wartime years brought considerable changes to the operation and maintenance of Gresley's express engines. The lightweight high-speed services disappeared, and were replaced by a pattern of heavy trains run at moderate speeds, with several intermediate stops. Locomotive and track maintenance became neglected, and the Pacifics, bred as racehorses, were forced to become adapted to a carthorse environment. In particular, the inherent weakness of the derived valve gear became obvious. Lack of mechanical fitters skilled in maintaining the gear led to complaints from the operating staff, and as mileage

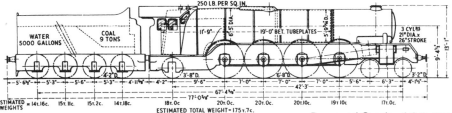

Proposed Gresley 4-8-2, 1939

between shoppings increased, so did the inability of the locomotives to exert their full power. It was in this general climate that Sir Nigel's untimely death occurred. His successor, Edward Thompson, soon made known his dislike for certain Gresley features, particularly the derived valve gear, and Gresley's lack of progress towards standardisation. As it happened, he had two opportunities to develop his idea for the largest engines, the first being in July 1942, when he submitted his ideas for rebuilding a 'P2' Mikado as a Pacific. The memorandum containing the proposal was in fact signed by the then Chief General Manager, Sir Charles Newton, and the recommendations were endorsed by the Board; so it cannot be said that Thompson acted alone. The Paper opened by explaining the virtues of locomotive standardisation and went on to point to the probability of defects in the Gresley derived motion, described as the '2 to 1 lever arrangement' after the characteristics of one of the main members of the derived mechanisms, and which led to overloading of the middle big end. A comprehensive report had been obtained, it was said, of breakdowns on the road due to failures of the Gresley gear, and this was supplemented by a report commissioned from Sir William Stanier. This was in fact based on an on-the-spot investigation by E. S. Cox, who in a very fair assessment of the position, and acknowledging that the gear was theoretically correct, found, perhaps not unexpectedly, that wear in the valve gear of the centre cylinder led to considerable inequality of output between the centre and outside cylinders, so much so that at high speeds the centre cylinder could develop considerably more power than either of the outside cylinders; this in turn placed more stress on an already weak design of big end.

As a result of these investigations, it was decided to suspend the building of locomotives with derived motion, thus leading to the cancellation of no fewer than 30 'V2s' outstanding on the 1941 programme. Dealing with the 'P2s', it was said that these were subject to frequent mechanical trouble, and it was decided to convert one of these to the 4-6-2 wheel arrangement with independent valve gear for the middle cylinder, which would overcome existing problems and provide information on which to base a design for a future heavy mixed traffic engine. To obtain sufficient clearance for the valve gear, the inside cylinder had to be moved well forward and made to drive on to the leading axle. A year later, in July 1943, approval was given for the conversion of the five remaining 'P2s', on the same lines as the first, which was reported as having proved 'entirely satisfactory'. At the same time — and this was Thompson's second opportunity to develop his mixed traffic Pacific — the Board agreed to the building of the last four outstanding 'V2s' as Pacifics. Wartime shortages precluded him from developing his own ideas entirely from scratch, and he was forced to concentrate on a design which made maximum use of existing components. It was probably this last constraint which led to the application of the short connecting rod of the 'P2' and 'V2' classes to a Pacific configuration to which it was ill-suited. His initial considerations also took in a de-streamlined 'A4', with divided drive and independent valve gear, in which design he was again forced to accept the short connecting rod by the circumstances of the time, although later on, when the shortcomings of this were known, he persisted with this feature even when he was able to build new locomotives. The placing of the outside cylinders behind the bogie wheels led to an inordinately long wheelbase, with frames and steam pipes prone to fracture, presenting an ungainly appearance, and one certainly not in the Gresley tradition. Anyway, Thompson converted the 'P2s' to a 6ft 2in Pacific design with a boiler shortened by 2ft, but with a longer smokebox and (adopting a Gresley feature) double blastpipe and chimney, and shorn of their streamlined casing. These rebuilds were followed by the Pacific version of the 'V2', in which, compared with the rebuilt 'P2s', the boiler was similar, but the cylinders and firegrate smaller, according with the 'V2' dimensions. When, after the war, Thompson was able to build new locomotives, based on his experience with these two versions of a 6ft 2in Pacific, there were reversions to the conventional dome and to the flat fronted spectacle plate, as though he had taken a dislike to these Gresley refinements, whilst another Gresley innovation, the rocking grate, was also abandoned. Smoke clearance problems arising from the soft exhaust called for immediate remedial treatment, and after initial experiments with small deflectors around the side of the chimney, full-sized side sheets were fitted to the smokebox. The first of this class, numbered 500 and given the classification 'A2', was named *Edward Thompson*, entering service only weeks before his retirement on 30 June 1946, and with a neat piece of numerical juggling becoming the two thousandth engine to be built at Doncaster. In these locomotives, the 50sq ft grate of the 'P2s' was reintroduced, and the 19in×26in cylinders of the 'A3'. With a 250lb/sq in boiler, they were powerful engines, tractive effort being 40,430lb.

As a prototype for his projected 6ft 8in Pacific, Thompson carried out a massive rebuilding of No 4470 *Great Northern* and what was virtually a new locomotive entered traffic in September 1945. Perhaps after a few years in office he considered that he had earned himself sufficient freedom of action to carry out the rebuild on his own responsibility, since he appears not to have told his Board officially of his proposals; he had possibly discussed it informally with the Locomotive Committee but the point had not been minuted. Alternatively, since he had the remit anyway to keep the locomotive stock in good order, he could defend his action by saying it was merely a reboilering, which the engine needed, and whilst it was in works the opportunity was taken to try out a new cylinder arrangement with independent valve gear for the centre cylinder on the lines already applied to the 'P2' conversions. However, although he intended his new 6ft 8in Pacific to be based on experience gained from the rebuilt No 4470, his time ran out before his ideas could be transformed into hardware. Moreover, the choice of *Great Northern* itself has been the subject of a great deal of controversy, but although it has been said that this engine was selected because it was in works at the time for major overhaul, so was No 2556 *Ormonde*, which could equally well have been the new prototype without raising so much discord. Despite representations by senior staff, Thompson persisted with *Great Northern* and may even have believed that in improving the locomotive — in his view — his action might have met with the approbation of Gresley. If so, this point of view has not met with the support of observers. The rebuild was unsatisfactory aesthetically, with its disproportionately long smokebox, cramped propulsion gear, and ill-proportioned cab perched high on the frames. After only two months, the cab side sheets were extended downwards, and full size smoke deflectors added. Nevertheless, after these modifications, apart from the higher running plate, the casual observer could be excused if he thought that the rear half of the engine still appeared as almost pure Gresley. But what could one make of the parentage of the front half? As one railwayman put it, if ever an engine came from the wrong side of the blanket, it was this one. To be fair, however, in its later life *Great Northern* settled down satisfactorily, and was well spoken of by operating men.

Arthur Peppercorn succeeded Thompson on 1 July 1946 and immediately set about restoring better proportions to the breed. With J. F. Harrison, then Assistant CME, and E. Windle, the Doncaster Chief Draughtsman, virtually responsible for design of the final LNER locomotives, steps were taken immediately to reshape the 6ft 2in Thompson 'A2' Pacifics, a number of which were currently under construction at Doncaster. Indeed, even before Peppercorn had assumed office, the drawing office was quietly working away on modifications. After 15 'A2s' had been completed to the Thompson specification (later to be reclassified 'A2/3') another 15 were built on more conventional lines which saw the outside cylinders restored to their position between the bogie wheels, but which retained the divided drive and three separate sets of Walschaerts valve gear. The steam collector, wedge shaped spectacle plate, and rocking grate were restored, but there was a strange reversion to a single blast pipe and chimney, later however replaced by a Kylchap double blast system in the last of the batch. The first of the new series of 'A2s' was numbered 525 and appropriately named *A. H. Peppercorn*, and was the last locomotive to be turned out from Doncaster before the onset of nationalisation. Altogether, 40 'A2s' were constructed or obtained from rebuilding — six (Nos 501-506) from rebuilds of the 'P2s', four (Nos 507-510) originally intended as 'V2s', 15 of the Thompson design (Nos 500, 511-524), and 15 by Peppercorn, (Nos 525-539). At one time it was thought that a further 20 would be ordered, but 6ft 8in 'A1s' were built instead. Consideration was also given to ordering 20 from Beyer Peacock, and this reached the tendering stage, but the firm were busy with export orders at the time and their price was reckoned to be too high.

After consideration of alternative profiles owing something to No 10000 and to the 'A4s', the final version of the LNER family of Pacifics was introduced in August 1948. This was a 6ft 8in design of classic outline, apart from the addition of large smoke deflecting plates, classed 'A1' and numbered 60114-62 in the British Railways style. This was the same classification that had been given to the very first series 26 years before, all of which were eventually rebuilt to the 'A3' specification, those unconverted by April 1945 being reclassed 'A10' in the interim. By an odd coincidence, Gresley's A1 No 1470 was completed by the GNR eight months before the formation of the LNER; Peppercorn's first 'A1' emerged eight months after the LNER had disappeared into the maelstrom of British Railways. The new class continued to be built at Doncaster and Darlington until the end of 1949, by which time no fewer than 49 had been put into traffic, several emerging from the works in LNER apple green livery. The 'A1' was undoubtedly a fine locomotive, well in the Gresley tradition, and still displaying many of the master's characteristics. The dimensions differed from those of the 'A4s' by the boiler being a foot shorter (2ft shorter than that of the 'A3s'), with a corresponding addition to the length of the combusion chamber, whilst the grate area was 50sq ft. The boiler was pressed to 250lb/sq in, the three cylinders were 19in×26in, and the tractive effort 37,397lb; 10in diameter piston valves were provided. The 'A1s' should have been good steamers, and they were, but they did not give such a good ride as the 'A4s', nor were they quite so economical, although they scored heavily on the question of maintenance, particularly five which were built new with Timken roller bearings on all axleboxes. The class averaged around 100,000 miles between heavy repairs, and the roller bearing examples even more, figures which were well above those for any competing class on British Railways. It is however ironic that the class, designed to haul 600ton trains at 60mph, shortly met with the BR policy to run lighter, more frequent, trains, so that they were not often exploited to their full potential.

The 'A1s' came on the scene too late for the 1948 locomotive exchanges; it would have been interesting to have compared their performance with that of the 'Duchess'. To obtain comparative data, R. C. Bond suggested that five 'Duchesses' should be sent to Kings Cross, and five 'A1s' to Camden, but this was not proceeded with. However during 1951-53 three of Haymarket's 'A1s' had spells at Polmadie shed, working on West Coast expresses as far south as Crewe, but no serious study seems to have been made of their performance during this period.

The 'A1s', then, were the last of the long sequence of LNER Pacifics, which even allowing for the Thompson vagaries, all followed a discernible pattern of development, commencing with GNR No 1470 *Great Northern* in April 1922 and ending with BR No 60162 *Saint Johnstoun* in December 1949, and totalling 203 in all, built or rebuilt in nine different classes. As a tribute to the lasting influence of their original designer, in his Presidential Address to the Institution of Locomotive Engineers in 1961, J. F. Harrison said of the 'A1': 'This is the kind of engine Sir Nigel Gresley would have designed had he still been alive'.

Gresley's interest in American practice was repeated in the early postwar years when a small team visited the USA to study current steam locomotive development over there. An important conclusion was that the steel firebox and the thermic siphon were bound to come, but an essential pre-requisite was the provision of feedwater of zero hardness. Also, a 4-8-4 prototype was recommended for development, with 6ft 8in coupled wheels, with the added proviso that a set of 6ft 4in wheels should be made, to afford data for both diameters, and, by interpolation, for 6ft 6in diameter. Preparations for an eight-coupled express locomotive had in fact reached the stage of outline drawings, prepared in 1946 before Thompson had retired, but whether these were serious considerations by the CME, or a long look into the future on the part of the drawing office, is not known. Three outlines were prepared, one of a 4-8-2 and two of 4-8-4 type; the main dimensions — not all of which were given — appeared to be the same, the only difference being the substitution of a pair of trailing axles, with 3ft 2in wheels, in place of the traditional single axle with 3ft 8in wheels. The 4-8-2 and one of the 4-8-4s appeared as a reversion to the original 'P2' profile, whilst the second 4-8-4 was streamlined on 'A4' lines. 6ft 8in wheels

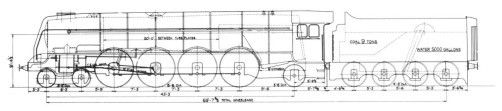

Outline of postwar 4-8-2, February 1946. *BR*

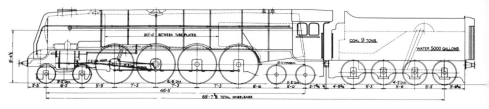

Outline of postwar 4-8-4, February 1946. *BR*

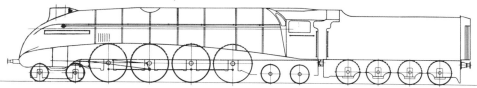

Outline of postwar streamlined 4-8-4, February 1946. *BR*

indicated that the locomotives were visualised as being employed on high speed services, whilst unlike the Gresley 4-8-2 proposal the maximum use was to be made of the wheelbase, the boiler being 20ft between tubeplates, and a large smokebox and a large combustion chamber incorporated. Harrison's own thoughts tended towards a 4-8-2 with 6ft 4in wheels (this being the optimum diameter in relation to the maximum piston speed then thought desirable) and an automatic stoker, to be followed by a Chapelon inspired 4-cylinder compound with a boiler pressed to 400lb/sq in.

Although the 'A1' was the last lineal descendent to exhibit the Gresley influence, this may be discerned to a certain extent in two other schools of locomotive design. O. H. V. Bulleid, who had joined the GNR in 1901 as a premium apprentice under H. A. Ivatt, had been closely associated with Gresley as his confidant and adviser for many years. Bulleid had been responsible for putting many ideas to his Chief, and had been in charge of several special projects, notably the 'P2' 2-8-2s. Nevertheless many of his suggestions were too unorthodox for Gresley, and after Bulleid had become CME of the Southern Railway in 1937, it came as no surprise that his 'Merchant Navy' Pacifics incorporated several novel features. They were of course much more Bulleid than Gresley, but they did follow Gresley precepts in their wide firebox, free steaming boiler, streamlined steam passages, and three cylinders all driving on to the centre axle. However the Bulleid Pacifics, although fast and powerful on their day, had a poor record for availability, and after Bulleid's retirement considerable pressure arose to modify them. R. A. Smeddle (previously at Darlington and later to be CMEE Western Region) was then Deputy to S. B. Warder, who had followed Bulleid as Southern Region CMEE, and he took the initiative. He gave instructions to R. G. Jarvis who had joined the Southern Region from the LMR, and who was then in charge of the Regional drawing office as Chief Technical Assistant (Locomotives), to the effect that drawings should be produced of the Bulleid Pacifics rebuilt on more conventional lines. Earlier, R. A. Riddles had suggested a rebuilding with two cylinders on the lines of the 'Britannias', but Jarvis found that it was possible to retain the 3-cylinder arrangement, even making use of the existing outside cylinders. By the time the proposals were ready,

H. H. Swift, Gresley's Assistant Electrical Engineer, had become CMEE Southern Region, and it was he who signed the submission for authority to be given for the rebuilding. So, we have the intriguing situation in which one of Gresley's erstwhile assistants built the controversial Southern Pacifics, and another was in charge when the rebuilding first commenced. It would be wrong however to credit any of the details of the redesign to Swift; this was carried through by Jarvis.

The standard British Railways designs, developed by a team under R. A. Riddles, owed much to LMS practice, as might be expected, having regard to the allegience of most of the design team. The standard locomotives followed certain principles quite foreign to the ideas of Gresley: the use of two cylinders on large locomotives, for example, and the adoption of the Belpaire firebox. Nevertheless, some details of Gresley practice can be discerned. The 'Britannia's' tapered boiler was dimensionally similar to that of the 'V2', although the wide firebox differed considerably; the 6ft 2in diameter coupled wheels of the BR Pacifics were based on an LNER dimension, whilst the 3-bar type of slidebar, applied to the largest standard classes, followed Gresley's introduction of the pattern many years before. Finally, the 'Britannia' chimney might well have been taken from a 'V2'.

In the last BR steam locomotive to be designed, No 71000 *Duke of Gloucester*, the power required, and the restrictions of the British loading gauge, meant that the engine had to be multi-cylindered: in LMS days this would have led to a 4-cylinder design, and E. S. Cox would have adopted this. But at the time the last word lay with Riddles, who on the advice of J. F. Harrison, then CMEE of the LMR, decided on a 3-cylinder layout, with the drive divided between the leading and centre axles. The boiler was based on that of the 'Duchess' class, with a 50sq ft grate; internal steam passages were fully streamlined, and a double blast pipe and chimney were fitted, but not the Kylchap cowls, although these were added in the 1980s reconstruction of No 71000. Following successful trials with a number of Class 5 4-6-0s fitted with Caprotti valve gear, previously applied by Gresley to certain of Robinson's 4-6 0s, this poppet valve system was also fitted to the 'Duke'. Unfortunately however the locomotive rarely lived up to its potential when running on the West Coast main line, and Harrison believed that the crews handling the 'Duke' did not apply the correct technique for firing such a large box, and thought that better performance would have been obtained on the Eastern Region by crews following the 'little and often' method adopted there. The cylinder efficiency was high, the difficulty lay in the back end, and had time permitted before the end of the steam era, the services of Rugby Testing Station would have been brought in to conduct a step-by-step investigation to identify and correct the precise problem area, and so to enable the 'Duke' to produce the performance expected of it.

As a final commentary on the benefits often obtained by an interchange of experience, an interesting exchange of personalities between Swindon and Doncaster took place in 1952, when K. J. Cook moved from Western Region to become CMEE Eastern and North Eastern Regions, and R. A. Smeddle, who had been at Darlington before spending a short time on the Southern, took Cook's place at Swindon. Cook brought Swindon optical lining-up technology to Doncaster, introducing a precision hitherto unknown; he also demonstrated that an inner big end bearing following Swindon practice, and maintained at frequent intervals, could eradicate the overheating which still plagued the Pacifics under certain conditions. On the Western Region, Smeddle continued with the introduction of high temperature superheat which had been initiated by Hawksworth and extended to a number of classes the improved draughting arrangements developed by S. O. Ell. However the double blastpipes applied to the 'Kings', 'Castles' and 'Counties' were plain, being based on two '2301' class chimneys, and could not be said to owe anything to Gresley.

Far left: Sir Nigel Gresley, CBE, DSc, MInstCE, MIMechE, MIEE. *Author's collection*

Left: William Whitelaw and Nigel Gresley at a Doncaster sports day. *T. Henry Turner*

Below: Sir Nigel Gresley and No 4498. *Author's collection*

"A Knight of the Iron Road"

SIR NIGEL GRESLEY, C.B.E.

President

INSTITUTION OF MECHANICAL ENGINEERS
1936-37

Above: Sir Nigel Gresley and his senior staff at the naming of No 4498. *IAL*

Left: 'The Speeder-up of the LNER'. *Author's collection*

Facing page, top: No 2003 *Lord President* leaving Waverley tunnel, Edinburgh. *A. C. Cawston*

Facing page, centre: No 2795 *Call Boy* passing Greenwood box, Hadley Wood with the up 'Flying Scotsman', September 1934. *Wethersett Collection/IAL*

Facing page, bottom: No 2511 *Silver King* passing Peterborough North with the up 'Silver Jubilee'. Until more 'A4s' were built the 'Jubilee' was normally hauled by one of the three 'silver' engines stationed at Kings Cross, No 2511 being the standby engine at Gateshead. *T. G. Hepburn/Rail Archive Stephenson*

Above: No 2555 *Centenary* passing Grantham
with the up 'Scarborough Flyer', August 1932.
T. G. Hepburn/Rail Archive Stephenson

Below: No 2544 *Lemberg* on a Leeds
Express leaving Grantham. *T. G.
Hepburn/Rail Archive Stephenson*

Below right: GNR No 461. The first
3-cylinder 2-8-0, with original conjugated
gear, 3-bar type slidebars and lightweight
crosshead. *IAL*

Above: No 2547 *Doncaster* on up non-stop 'Flying Scotsman' near Finsbury Park, June 1928. *F.R.Hebron/Rail Archive Stephenson*

Below: GNR No 1633. One of the original 2-6-0s with small boiler, 2-bar type slide bars with heavy crosshead and piston tailrods. *IAL*

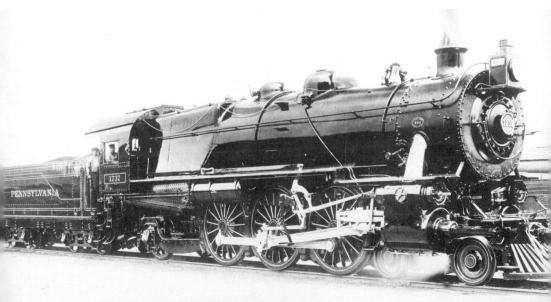

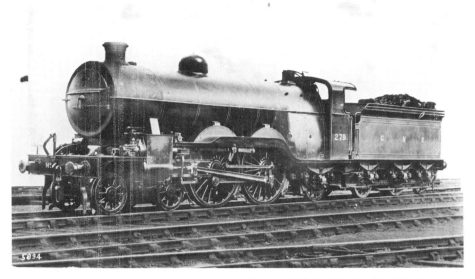

Top left: GNR No 1001. The second large boiler 3-cylinder 2-6-0, with later version of conjugated gear, and machined alloy rods. *Crown Copyright, National Railway Museum, York*

Centre left: GNR No 1473. One of the first production batch of Pacifics, later named *Solario* after the winner of the 1925 St Leger. *Real Photos*

Bottom left: Pennsylvania RR 'K4s' No 1737, the first of the class. Note similarities, and differences, compared with Gresley Pacifics. *Real Photos*

Above: GNR No 279. Modified by Gresley to obtain experience with 4-cylinder drive. *Real Photos*

Below: No 2750 *Papyrus*. One of the first batch built new as Class A3. Achieved 108mph in 1935. *Crown Copyright, National Railway Museum, York*

Above: No 4473 *Solario* on 4pm down express approaching Greenwood box, September 1934. *Wethersett Collection/IAL*

Right: No 4470 *Great Northern*, on a down express emerging from Oakleigh Park tunnel, April 1931. Original Class A1 but with long travel valves. *Wethersett Collection/IAL*

Below: No 2404 *City of Ripon*. Raven Pacific rebuilt with 'A1' boiler and firebox. *L&GRP, courtesy David & Charles*

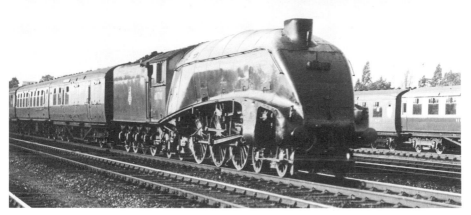

Top: Class W1 No 10000 in original compound form, with water-tube boiler. *IAL*

Below: No 2001 *Cock o' the North* in original condition, 1934. *Crown Copyright, National Railway Museum, York*

Above: BR No 60700 rebuilt as a 3-cylinder simple and 'A4' profile, but with the fairings over the wheels removed. New Southgate, August 1952. *Wethersett Collection/IAL*

Top: No 2003 *Lord President* as built with streamlined front. *Crown Copyright, National Railway Museum, York*

Below: No 2512 *Silver Fox* on up 'Silver Jubilee' at Marshmoor, June 1937. Name painted on side of boiler cladding above stainless steel fox emblem. *Wethersett Collection/IAL*

Above: No 4491 *Commonwealth of Australia* in blue livery for working the 'Coronation'. Stainless steel characters, coat of arms on cab sides. *Crown Copyright, National Railway Museum, York*

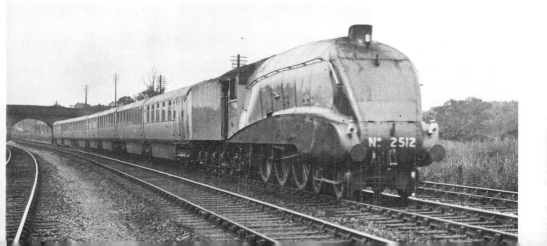

Top: No 4498 *Sir Nigel Gresley* on up 'Flying Scotsman', June 1938, with new coaching stock. *Wethersett Collection/IAL*

Above: No 4771 *Green Arrow* as turned out in 1936 in green livery. *IAL*

Below: No 4772 at Neasden, October 1937. LNER green but needing to be cleaned. *Wethersett Collection/IAL*

Top: BR No 60964 *The Durham Light Infantry.* 'V2' in BR green at Gateshead, October 1961. Modified with new cylinders and outside steampipes. *P. J. Robinson*

Bottom: No 4470 *Great Northern*, after rebuilding by Thompson in 1945. Royal blue livery, plain chimney, short cab sides. *IAL*

Below: No 508 *Duke of Rothesay.* Thompson Pacific version of 'V2' as Class A2/1. *IAL*

Chapter 4

Secondary Passenger Locomotives

During his time with the Great Northern, Nigel Gresley had no real need to develop a new design for a four-coupled passenger locomotive, but in 1914 he did in fact give consideration to what might have been a powerful 4-4-0. Only a wheelbase and weight diagram has survived, from which it may be deduced that the leading dimensions would have been similar to those of the contemporary GCR 'Directors'. Although the proposal got as far as receiving the approval of the Civil Engineer, the proposal was not taken further; instead, Gresley looked carefully at the details of Ivatt's large Atlantics with a view to improving their efficiency. Primarily he paid attention to better superheating, and after a number of trials the Robinson 32-element superheater became standardised. In addition there was a gradual substitution of piston for slide valves on those engines which had not been so fitted from new. These improvements transformed the Atlantics from a powerful though sluggish class into one capable of brilliant performance. Other interesting experiments took place on GNR No 279, which was rebuilt in 1915 with four cylinders, to gain experience with this arrangement for possible application to the embryo Pacific, and on No 1419, to which a booster was fitted in 1923, this being removed in 1935, after limited success.

At grouping the LNER possessed 263 4-6-0s, 241 4-4-2s and 920 4-4-0s, of no fewer than 71 different classes. 206 of the 4-6-0s were engaged on mixed traffic or freight work. Such a heterogeneous collection of locomotives could not last, one would think, but even 10 years later only 32 4-6-0s, 2 4-4-2s, and 193 4-4-0s had been withdrawn — a tribute to the longevity of the typical British locomotive, but also a commentary on the inability of the LNER to fund up-to-date replacements.

On 2 January 1923, the second day of the LNER's existence, the

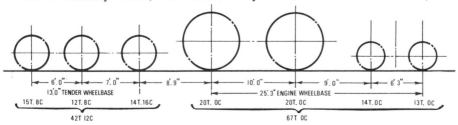

Wheelbase and weight diagram of proposed 4-4-0, 1914. *Author's Collection*

Superintendents of each Area met to discuss their needs for new locomotives. The Great Northern and North Eastern representatives expected more Pacifics to cover their main express services, but the Great Eastern, whilst stating that more powerful locomotives were needed, agreed with the Great North of Scotland that a prerequisite was the strengthening of the permanent way. The Great Central asked for 10 more 'Directors', but this was not pressed on the understanding that Ivatt Atlantics would become available for GC services as they became displaced by Pacifics on the Great Northern. However, on the North British, the need was urgent as, of large wheeled engines, only two Atlantics and five 'Scotts' had been built since the war; other new construction had been delayed pending the grouping. Consequently the NB request was for five more Atlantics and 10 'Scotts', but despite William Whitelaw's translation from the North British to the LNER, no further passenger locomotives were to be constructed to NBR designs.

In later years, with money available, a standard 6ft 2in 4-6-0 would have been mass-produced to meet many of these varying requests, but this was not how the solution was seen in 1923. Gresley's response to the urgent calls upon his resources was to request Darlington to prepare a design for a 3-cylinder 4-4-0, but even this was to take second place to a modern 0-6-0. Doncaster was occupied with a number of proposals, and a 3-cylinder 4-6-0 capable of meeting the weight limits of the Great Eastern was included. However the North British could not wait for the new 4-4-0; something was needed now. Gresley concluded that his Pacifics would remove any desire for more NB Atlantics, whilst in his view the Robinson 'Directors', LNER Class D11, were the best of the pre-grouping 4-4-0s; possibly he was reminded of his own abortive proposal of 1914. The 'Directors' possessed a larger boiler than the 'Scotts', and although he did not care for the Belpaire firebox, time did not permit a redesign. 24 'D11s' were provided in 1924 for the North British, the original outline being later improved by the omission of the valances over the coupled wheels, whilst a happy decision was to paint names on the splashers in NB fashion; splendid names in fact, from Sir Walter Scott's writings. So, whilst the new Southern Scottish Area didn't get 'Scott' engines at least they got 'Scott' names. These 'D11s' were numbered 6378-6401, and to speed delivery the order was divided between Kitson of Leeds and Armstrong Whitworth, each company supplying 12. Strangely, it was the arrival of Pacifics on the Great Northern which indirectly provided additional motive power for the Northern Scottish Area, as the Great North of Scotland was now titled. The Pacifics took work from the Ivatt Atlantics; this released GN 4-4-0s, the best of which, the 15 'D1s' of 1911, were sent in 1925 to the North British, which in turn parted with a number of its elderly 'D31s' to Aberdeen. By such palliatives was the newly formed LNER to make the most of the varied locomotive fleet it had inherited, postponing the construction of new locomotives at the expense of higher maintenance costs in the shops, and frustration amongst the running staff. (There was anything but a warm welcome for the 'D1s' on the North British, where they were regarded as rough riding, and with insufficient cab protection against the Scottish winters. Nor was their vacuum brake appreciated, and all had to be fitted with Westinghouse braking equipment.)

Gresley's own 4-4-0s eventually appeared in 1927, classified 'D49'. Although never really in the limelight they performed adequately on secondary services in the North Eastern and Southern Scottish Areas. They comprised an amalgam of the boiler and firebox designed the previous year for the 'J38/39' 0-6-0s, together with Gresley's three cylinders and derived valve gear. Tractive effort was 21,556lb. One of his principles had to be breached, however: the drive was on to the front coupled axle. However, on a 4-4-0, this had to be accepted, but it possessed the advantage of allowing the conjugated valve gear to be installed behind the cylinders instead of in front of them, as was the case in those classes in which the drive was on to the centre axle. The first 36 members of the class were named after Shires, later examples with rotary cam poppet valves being given the names of Hunts; two 'Shires' which had been built experimentally with these valves were later renamed as 'Hunts'. The 'D49s' in fact were subjected to a number of variations of poppet valve gear, described in more detail in Chapter 11. The class eventually totalled 76, all from Darlington, the last in 1935. Apart from a batch numbered 2753-60, they took vacant numbers in the 200s and 300s.

In the meantime, Doncaster was making little progress in producing a 4-6-0 for the Great Eastern. It was believed that Gresley would have welcomed the opportunity to produce a 3-cylinder equivalent of the 'Castle', to show C. B. Collett that he too could build a powerful 4-6-0. But a 'Castle' was out of the question on the Great Eastern, with the weak state of underbridges and track brought into the LNER at grouping. The Drawing Office was thus constrained on the one hand by the need to keep down the weight on the coupled wheels, and the length, so that any new engine could be accommodated by the existing turntables and laybyes, and on the other hand to keep to Gresley's principles of three cylinders, derived valve gear and undivided drive on to the centre axle. The first attempted design was calculated to have been too heavy, the second was too long. But in the meantime the GER traffic problem was becoming exacerbated by the provision of new and heavier rolling stock, particularly for the 'Hook Continental'. By the summer of 1927 matters had reached crisis point, and a meeting was convened by the Chief General Manager, which the CME did not attend. A recommendation was made that 20 'B12s' should be ordered as a matter of urgency, but for once the normally acquiescent Locomotive Committee did not agree. The Officers were told that they must do better than that, and whilst 10 'B12s' were authorised, it was left that a new, improved, design must be produced even if it meant going to an outside contractor. So, a design and construct contract was given to the North British Locomotive Company, as a result of which the 'B17' 'Sandringham' class was produced, with a boiler pressed to 200lb/sq in, three 17½in × 26in cylinders and tractive effort of 25,380lb. On paper meeting the requirement for a maximum axle loading of 17 tons, this was achieved in part by departing from the principle of undivided drive, the middle cylinder driving on to the leading coupled axle. Nevertheless, the class exhibited Gresley lineaments and has always been regarded as one of his products. How much design was in fact carried out by NBL can only be conjectured; the boiler owed a good deal to Darlington practice, a recognisable external feature being the short straps to the smokebox door hinges. The first 10 took some time to settle down, suffering from frame fractures in their early days, but the class was soon multiplied by further construction at Darlington. The first batches, Nos 2800-47, bore the names of country estates, but the later examples up to No 2872, were named after football clubs; some names are changed in later years, however. The 'Footballers', intended originally for the Great Central, were given Group

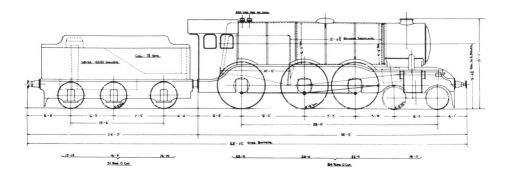

Drawing of 4-6-0 proposed in 1935 although it is believed that the outline may have originated earlier. *BR*

Standard tenders; until then, the class had been provided with shorter tenders of Great Eastern pattern, to minimise the overall length. Despite the initial involvement of the North British Locomotive Company, no further orders were placed with this firm. They undoubtedly considered this to be less than fair, particularly when an order (for the last 11, as it happened) went to Robert Stephenson & Co.

One of the most interesting of Gresley's proposals which did not get beyond the drawing board was a larger 4-6-0. How far his ideas had progressed when the then current project was handed over to the North British Loco Co is not known, but it is possible that having regard to improvements in design technique since the exchanges with the 'Castles' in 1925, and to a lessening of restrictions on the Great Eastern, a larger 4-6-0 than the 'B17' could have been accepted there in the early 1930s. Spencer has described a later outline which would have had a Pacific front end arrangement, taper boiler, three $18\frac{1}{2}$in×26in cylinders, and a tractive effort of 31,200lb, little short of that of the 'Castles'. This proposal was discussed around the period that the 'V2' was being planned and at one time it was thought that the two might be developed concurrently, having regard to the limited route availability of the 'V2'. But the 'B18' (if that was to have been its classification) would have had an axle weight of 22 tons, which would have kept if off the Great Eastern for many years. Possibly it was regarded as a hedge against the 'V2' not fulfilling its promise, particularly if the 2-6-2s leading pony truck was found to be unsuitable for high speeds. However the 'V2' soon showed its capabilities, and not only was the large 4-6-0 not proceeded with, but in 1936 proposals to build a further 32 'B17s' were cancelled in favour of 28 more 'V2s'.

Meanwhile, the 10 'B12s' had been delivered in 1928 by Beyer Peacock; as an afterthought Gresley had required them to be fitted with Lentz poppet valves, as experiments with other engines of this class appeared to indicate that this modification brought about an improvement in efficiency. However the makers had not included this in their contract price, and a serious disagreement ensued. Harsh words were said, and strong letters written. Indeed, court proceedings were threatened, but in the end settlement was reached by the LNER paying £1,500, half the Beyer Peacock claim.

By 1931, track conditions on the GER had improved to the extent that a higher axle weight could be accepted on certain routes. Edward Thompson was now Mechanical Engineer at Stratford, and with Gresley's authority transformed the 'B12s' by producing a rebuild with a larger boiler, round topped firebox, and longer travel valve gear; eventually no fewer than 54 were rebuilt in this way, classified 'B12/3'. As a result of the rebuilding the traditional Great Eastern outline was replaced by one unmistakably Gresley. Commencing in 1931, unrebuilt members of the class were transferred in small numbers to the Northern Scottish Area, where their low axle loading and relatively high power made them well suited to the routes centred on Aberdeen. From 1943, Thompson began to provide these with new boilers and round topped fireboxes, but retaining the original main dimensions. Nine were rebuilt in this way, classified 'B12/4'.

As well as a number of the class being fitted with Lentz valves, many were provided with the French ACFI feedwater heating system. Neither of these adaptations proved successful in the long run, and were eventually removed, the poppet valves being replaced by conventional piston valves.

Another Great Eastern class selected for modernisation was the 'Claud Hamilton' 4-4-0. Originally appearing in 1900, these had been provided from new with round topped fireboxes, but A. J. Hill had later replaced these by the Belpaire type; also, he developed a larger version of the class, dubbed the 'Super-Clauds', which appeared in 1923. In antithesis of Gresley's policy, Belpaire boxes continued to replace the original round topped variety until all had been converted by 1931. However it was then decided that a general modernisation scheme should be introduced, and again during Thompson's time at Stratford, a reboilered version with round topped firebox was developed, bringing a further Gresley outline to the scene.

Another pre-grouping class which was subjected to experiment was the Raven 3-cylinder Atlantic, Class C7. In association with A. C. Stamer at Darlington, representatives of the class were fitted with Dabeg or ACFI feedwater heaters, or Lentz poppet valves, whilst two were provided with boosters and were articulated with their tenders, for better riding. All these modifications were subsequently removed.

Following Stamer's retirement at the end of 1933, Thompson was promoted from Stratford to be Mechanical Engineer, North Eastern Area, at Darlington, but without Stamer's title of Assistant Chief Mechanical Engineer, which was allowed to lapse. Had the Grouping not taken place, Thompson would probably have achieved the position of CME of the North Eastern Railway, and undoubtedly he felt keenly the frustration of occupying Raven's old office without enjoying the CME's freedom of action. This was probably exacerbated at the end of 1935 by the removal to Doncaster of the Darlington capability to design new locomotives, leaving only a minimal drawing office to deal with local matters. Nevertheless, under Gresley's general direction, Thompson gave attention to two North Eastern designs — the mixed traffic 'B16' 4-6-0 and the 'D20' 4-4-0. The LNER classification 'D20' masked the identity of the celebrated North Eastern 'R' class, and one was rebuilt in 1936 with long travel valves. The running plate was partly raised, with the Darlington quadrant form of curve, but surprisingly no real effort was made to bring the profile more into line with other LNER classes. It retained its small boiler and smokebox and remained distinctly a North Eastern locomotive, which, it has been said, did not please Gresley. Three more of the class later had their valve system modernised in the same way, but without the alteration to the running plate. Both Gresley and Thompson, when CME, considered major improvements to the 'C7' Atlantics. Gresley's idea was to convert them to utilise Walschaerts valve gear, with conjugated motion for the inside cylinder, as on his rebuilds of the 'B16s', whilst Thompson briefly considered whether they could be more fundamentally rebuilt with two 20in×26in inside cylinders. Neither of these proposals resulted in more than a drawing office exercise.

The only Great Central passenger class which Gresley selected for improvement was the largest of the Robinson 4-6-0s, the 'Valour' class, LNER 'B3', four of which were fitted with Caprotti valve gear in efforts to reduce fuel consumption. None of the Scottish passenger locomotives were the subject of improvement, apart from minor boiler redesign, and the application of superheating in selected instances.

The large NB Atlantics were withdrawn in the 1930s but determined efforts were made to save one for preservation. No 9875 *Midlothian* was selected, after it had been withdrawn and scrapping commenced. New connecting and coupling rods were made and the engine returned to traffic, but with the outbreak of war it was finally withdrawn and broken up. The two most modern 4-4-0 designs, the 'Scotts' and 'Glens', virtually identical except for their wheel diameters, were left alone to continue their everyday duties. They were capable locomotives, within their limitations, and although it is believed that in 1939 plans were being considered for their rejuvenation, any such ideas were lost with the onset of the war.

So, it can be seen that by rebuilding or improving half-a-dozen pre-grouping classes, Gresley was able to maintain a fleet of second line passenger locomotives capable of meeting the needs of the period. Indeed, certain of these, the superheated 'C1s' and the 'B12/3s' in particular, were as important in their own way as his own two designs. Moreover, the continued employment of pre-grouping classes precluded the more widespread use of his own locomotives. The 'D49' 4-4-0s were stationed in the North Eastern and Southern Scottish Areas for their entire existence, apart from trials, as No 245 *Lincolnshire* was stationed at Kings Cross for a few months soon after it had entered service, demonstrating that in capable hands it could produce a performance as competent as that of a good Atlantic. On the other hand, the 'B17s' remained almost wholly on the Great Eastern, and to a lesser extent the Great Central, sections. A small number were stationed at Doncaster for a while, but were used mainly on cross-country services. Twice, batches were proposed for the North Eastern Area, but the class had never been welcomed there, and relief was expressed when first 'K3s' and later 'V2s', were provided instead. So, Gresley's two intermediate classes were mainly seen in different halves of the system — the 'D49s' north, and the 'B17s' south, of York.

Thompson's often reported desire to simplify Gresley's designs took the form, in the classes under review, of an inside-cylinder rebuild of the 'D49', and a 2-cylinder version of the 'B17'. One of the 'Hunts', No 365 *The Morpeth*, was in fact converted to inside-cylinder operation, and there seems to have been no reason why the locomotive, rebuilt on classic lines, should not have performed well. But this appears not to have been the case, and little information was released about the rebuild, reclassified simply as 'D', it being withdrawn in 1952 following a collision. The Darlington shape of the footplating, and the heavy appearance of the front end detracted from its looks. Perhaps however it was not unlike a 'D11' with a round topped firebox, a conversion would have been relatively simple during Gresley's day, employing the 'D49/J39' boiler — and one which certainly occurred to Thompson. A further variety of 4-4-0 was considered by Thompson, when CME, in the shape of a lightweight version with 6ft 2in wheels, for working over routes of severe weight restrictions, such as the line over Stainmore to Tebay. But nothing of this was contained in his later, published, standardisation proposals, which referred only to conversion of the 'D49s'.

The standardised replacement of the great majority of the LNER secondary passenger and mixed traffic tender engines, would, in the Thompson regime, be the 'B1' 6ft 2in 4-6-0, discussed in the next chapter. However he saw some continuing employment for existing locomotives rebuilt virtually as 'B1s' with larger driving wheels, and in this category a Robinson 'B3' (No 6166) was converted into a 'B3/3' at Gorton, and 10 'B17s' into 'B2s' at Darlington. These rebuilds, although distinguished by different classification, were virtually identical, but there seems to have been no exceptional performance or fuel saving improvement which might have justified such extensive rebuilding. A cheaper conversion was the fitting of the 225lb/sq in 'B1'-type boiler to the 'B17', which, retaining its 3-cylinder arrangement, seemed to be the better locomotive. Most of the class received this type of boiler eventually, becoming Class B17/6.

As a postscript to this chapter, it is worth observing that the LNER never seemed to achieve a successful locomotive policy for the main Great Eastern services. Hampered for many years by restrictions on the use of heavier locomotives, the best that could be done was to introduce the 'Sandringhams' and the rebuilt 'B12/3s', which whilst competent in many ways did not possess the power to cope adequately with the heaviest loads of the 1930s, reflecting the growing prosperity of East Anglia and the importance of the traffic between Parkeston Quay and the Continent. By the end of the decade the track on the main lines had been uprated to permit a 20ton axle load, which still precluded the use of Pacifics and 'V2s' apart from the 'A1s' of Gresley's original design, and these would probably have been forbidden because of their length. (An exception was made in the case of the 'K3s', a few of which appeared at Stratford in 1938.)

Thompson's standardisation plans only offered the 'B1', which was no real improvement on the 'B17', and both he and Peppercorn appeared to be waiting further upgrading of the track to allow a 22ton axle load, since nothing between the 'B1' and the 'A1/A2' was contemplated in their forward plans.

The matter was not resolved until BR days, when the obvious claims of the Great Eastern were so impressed on the top management that the first 'Britannias' (with an axle load of 20 tons) were drafted to East Anglia, a class long awaited and which at last enabled adequate locomotive power to be deployed on the main services out of Liverpool Street.

Chapter 5

Mixed Traffic Locomotives

Patrick Stirling had recognised the value of a locomotive capable of hauling fast goods trains, as well as secondary passenger and excursion working, by introducing an 0-4-2 class with 5ft 7in wheels as far back as 1867, and no fewer than 154 were built to the same general design. Although adequate for the purpose when they first appeared, the design continued in production for some 20 years, and the last examples were virtually obsolescent as soon as they were built. But no new mixed traffic class was to appear for many years, as Ivatt's primary task was to provide the Great Northern with more powerful passenger locomotives. Although he considered plans for a 5ft 8in compound 2-6-2 with a boiler similar to that of the large Atlantic (and in which it is believed that the young Bulleid had a hand), this did not proceed, and his eventual mixed traffic locomotive was much less of a step forward; in fact it was no more than a 0-6-0 with 5ft 8in coupled wheels. However this was an attempt to provide a class capable of dealing with the fast freight traffic which was growing rapidly in the early 1900s, with long through hauls from York and Manchester to Kings Cross, and for which it was the custom to use passenger engines, Atlantics and even Singles. With its lack of guiding wheels, a 0-6-0 was not ideal for such traffic, but nevertheless a further batch of 10 was built, this time with superheaters, in 1912. Authorisation for these had been obtained by Ivatt before he retired, and Gresley took no steps to alter the design, but no more were to be built.

Instead, in just under a year after he had assumed control, the first of Gresley's new designs emerged from Doncaster, his outside-cylindered 2-6-0 GNR No 1630, intended specifically for fast freight and mixed traffic duties. To design and construct an entirely new locomotive in such a short period was very good going, and one wonders whether in fact the conception and perhaps even some of the design had been worked on in private whilst Gresley was still Carriage and Wagon Superintendent, but in possession of Ivatt's confidential advice concerning his forthcoming retirement, and the likelihood of Gresley becoming his successor. The boiler diameter of No 1630, 4ft 8in, was the same as that of the last Ivatt 0-6-0s, and the tube and superheater arrangements were similar although of course the 2-6-0s boiler was longer, with a superheater, and the heating surface and grate area larger. So, possibly production of the 2-6-0 was expedited by following this existing boiler design.

The first of the class was followed early in 1913 by a further nine, the batch being constructed concurrently with a series of 0-6-0s — first, the balance of the Ivatt 5ft 8in batch, and later a number of his 5ft 2in class for short haul freight duty, to which Gresley made minor improvements. In 1914 an improved 2-6-0 appeared, with a recognisably larger 5ft 6in boiler possessing 2,070sq ft heating surface, the tractive effort remaining unchanged at 22,100lb, although this was slightly increased in LNER days when the 170lb/sq in to which the boilers were pressed was raised to 180lb. Twenty of the 2-6-0s emerged from Doncaster in 1914, GNR Nos 1640-59, LNER Class K2. They were followed by a further 20 for which the order had been placed with Beyer Peacock, but wartime difficulties intervened and the locomotives were completed by the North British Loco Co, the GNR providing the tenders. Finally, 25 came from Kitson of Leeds, in 1920/21, to bring the running numbers up to 1704.

Experience with the 'K2s' showed Gresley the possibilities of further development of the 2-6-0 type, and in 1917 he considered enlarging the 20in×26in cylinders of the 'K2' to 20in×28in, whilst maintaining the same boiler dimensions. This would have increased the tractive effort to 23,800lb, but having regard to the evident success of 3-cylinder propulsion as applied to his 2-8-0 GNR No 461, he decided to develop his 2-6-0 on similar lines, at the same time providing a still larger boiler. The result was GNR No 1000, LNER Class K3, which emerged from Doncaster in 1920 and was soon followed by nine others. As a class they created the greatest interest when they first appeared at Kings Cross, particularly as their introduction was followed by the 1921 coal strike and its consequential 600ton trains, with which the 'K3s' coped admirably. Their 6ft boiler provided a heating surface of 2,308sq ft whilst the three 18½in×26in cylinders and tractive effort of 30,032lb made the 'K3' the most powerful eight wheeled locomotive built, up until then, for a British railway. Other novel features introduced with this class were Ross 'pop' safety valves, then new to a Great Northern class, the three-bar type slide bars and lightweight crosshead introduced on 2-8-0 No 461, and machined alloy rods, later to be applied to Gresley's Pacifics. These components contributed to a reduction in the weight of the reciprocating parts to half that of the 'K2s', and also lessened the amount of wheel balancing required. Nevertheless, the 'K3s', like their predecessors, were notorious for rough riding, especially when in a rundown condition.

Although high axle loading kept the 'K3s' away from the Great Eastern section and several parts of Scotland, including the West Highland line, they soon penetrated the main lines of the other LNER constituents. The first orders for a Gresley design to be placed at Darlington resulted in the continuous production of 60 'K3s' in 1924/5, which apart from having cut-down boiler mountings to bring the class within the Composite Load Gauge, differed from the original Doncaster batch by being provided with NER cabs with low side windows instead of the GNR cutaway cab. Later these, and the original series, were provided with LNER pattern double side window cabs with the windows immediately beneath the cab roof. Twenty more were built at Darlington and others by Armstrong Whitworth, North British Loco Co and Robert Stephenson until the last appeared in 1937, by which time the class totalled 193. The running numbers were anything but systematic, mainly filling gaps in the North Eastern series, but the first 10 (Nos 4000-9) and the final 20 (Nos 3813-3832) were included in the Great Northern block of numbers.

Allocation of new 'K3s' to the Great Northern permitted a number of 'K2s' to be posted away, some to the Great Eastern, and some to Scotland, but in particular 13 used on the West Highland were given names of Scottish lochs and were later provided with single side window cabs to keep out the worst of the weather. The 'Glens' which were then the main source of motive power had an unassisted limit of 190 tons to Fort William, and this was increased to 220 tons, or another corridor coach, for a 'K2'.

An interesting experiment employing a water tube boiler operating at 300lb/sq in, allied to the 'K3' cylinders and mechanism, was considered in July 1931. By this time the 'Hush-hush' No 10000 had been in service for a year, and Gresley would have become well aware of its deficiencies. Was the application of a water-tube boiler with a lower working pressure and simple instead of compound propulsion in a smaller locomotive thought to have been more likely to succeed than in the massive 4-6-4? Perhaps the proposal was little more than a desk exercise; at any rate, nothing more has been discovered on the subject.

A further development of the 'K3' class was projected when two locomotives described as 'K3 improved' were authorised in January 1932 as part of the building programme for that year. The proposal maintained the 'K3' boiler and firebox, but with the cylinders enlarged to 19in×26in and the coupled wheels to 6ft 2in. Evidently since no more steam raising capacity was to be provided, the intention was to permit higher output and increased speed over relatively short distances. Apart from the complete absence of a dome, necessitated by the higher pitch of the boiler to clear the coupled wheels, the main external distinction of the 'K3 improved' was articulation of the locomotive with its tender, resulting in effect in a 2-6-4-4 wheel arrangement. This unusual concept, springing from Gresley's successful application of articulation to coaching stock, was contemporary with his conversion of two North Eastern Atlantics to booster operation, in which the locomotives and tenders were similarly articulated. Presumably, having regard to the rough riding which characterised the 'K3s', particularly at speed, the expectation was that the 'K3 improved' would be a better riding vehicle. However drawbacks soon became apparent in the booster fitted 'C9s', and in any case there

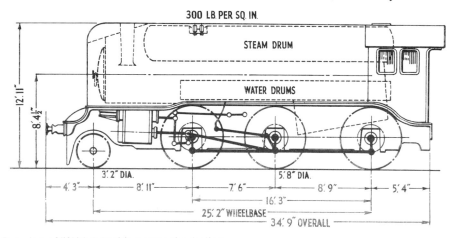

Drawing of 'K3' 2-6-0 with water tube boiler.

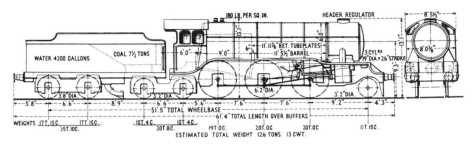

Drawing of 'K3 improved', authorised in 1932.

was a severe cutback in locomotive construction in 1932/3. When a building programme was next submitted, Gresley had raised his sights somewhat, and the 'V2' was on the horizon; consequently the 'K3 improved' was quietly forgotten. Nevertheless the proposal had reached the stage of an order on Darlington Works, and the locomotives had been allocated the numbers 1339 and 1399, to be taken instead by two of a later batch of 'K3s'.

An interesting unfulfilled proposal of this period was a 2-8-0 based on the '02', but with 5ft 2in coupled wheels and a special boiler tapering from 5ft 6in at the firebox end to 5ft at the smokebox. The objective was to produce a locomotive for the West Highland which would have a tractive effort 50% higher than the 'K2', but it was soon discovered that the locomotive would have been too long for the turntables and too heavy for the bridges. The matter was looked at once more, using the 2-6-0 wheel arrangement again, but with 5ft 2in wheels and with the 'K3' cylinders supplied with steam from a considerably smaller boiler than was fitted to that class. The first of the new locomotives, classed 'K4', had a 180lb/sq in boiler for a few months after entering service, but this was soon raised to 200lb, the tractive effort working out at 36,600lb. Six locomotives to this design were built at Darlington between 1937 and 1939, numbered 3441-46, and given splendid names appropriate to the Western Highlands. No 3442 *The Great Marquess* has been preserved and is owned by Lord Garnock. The 'K4s' were allowed to take 300 tons unassisted to Fort William, but were not altogether popular with their crews as they were prone to slipping and their smaller coupled wheels added to the inherent roughness of ride suffered by all the Gresley 2-6-0s, particularly on the level section of the line between Glasgow and Helensburgh, where higher speeds were customary. Nevertheless they were regarded as successful until lower maintenance standards resulting from wartime conditions brought the inevitable problems.

The LNER's most renowned mixed traffic locomotives were of course the 'V2s', first introduced in 1936 and built in quantity until 1944. They replaced the 'K3s' in the building programme, but with their superior capability they are rightly regarded as amongst the 'Big Engines'. Consequently they are discussed in Chapter 3.

Gresley's last new design was his smaller 2-6-2, Class V4, which was his personal response to the GWR 'Halls' and the LMS 'Black Fives', turned out in quantity in the 1930s. But there were significant differences in conception, not only in the wheel arrangement. The other railways' 4-6-0s were straightforward 2-cylinder locomotives with 6ft coupled wheels, and whilst of a good route availability were by no means go-anywhere machines. The 'V4' was conceived as a lightweight, employing penchants such as three cylinders, derived valve gear for the inside cylinder, wide firebox and tapered boiler, with the use of alloy steels for boiler drum and coupling rods contributing to weight reduction. It was a costly locomotive to build and maintain, but its designer's expectation was that the advantages deriving from its fuel efficiency, high performance and wide route availability would more than offset other expenses. Preliminary considerations of the 'V4' in 1939 included a note that if it was to be used on the Tebay branch, $14\frac{1}{2}$ tons would be the maximum axle load permitted. This constraint was soon discarded as being impossible to meet and the eventual design had an axle loading of 17 tons. The taper boiler was pressed to 250lb/sq in, and the 5ft 8in coupled wheels and 15in×26in cylinders produced a tractive effort of 27,420lb; grate area was 28.5sq ft and heating surface, 1,800sq ft. Before the final design was approved, consideration had been given to a 300lb/sq in boiler and 14in×26in cylinders, but this was soon rejected, possibly as being too much of a step forward. Perhaps this higher pressure was looked at in conjunction with a steel firebox, as the second 'V4' was provided with a firebox fabricated from welded steel and incorporating a siphon, following American practice, to improve water circulation around the firebox.

Unfortunately the design came at the wrong time, as the war was about to commence, and whilst the need for the new class was clear enough, and under peace time conditions adequate attention might have been given to maintenance, this was not to be the case. Nevertheless in January 1940 authority was given for two 'V4s', one for the Great Eastern and one for Scotland. They were described as 'an experimental type which it is hoped will solve the problem of passenger and freight workings on sections of the line where heavier engines are not permitted owing to engineering restrictions'. No 3401 was completed at Doncaster in February 1941 and appropriately named *Bantam Cock*; the second, No 3402, came out the following month. No 3401 earned very good reports on test runs when new, on such varied duties as express working between Doncaster and Leeds, and Liverpool Street and Norwich, as well as mineral hauls in Scotland. Both locomotives were ultimately stationed north of the Border, where the soft water was kinder to No 3402's steel firebox, but after four years this was replaced by a conventional copper box. Most of their working life was spent on the West Highland, where they gave their crews a better ride than the 2-6-0s. However they were limited to a trailing load of 250 tons, 50 tons less than the 'K4s', which had been specially built for the West Highland, and which were never equalled by any other class to run on that line. The two 'V4s' were Gresley's last class, and had hardly turned a wheel before he passed away. It is hard to say to what extent they would have been multiplied had he continued in office, but no firm proposals had been made to add to the class in a future programme.

Of the LNER's constituent companies, the North Eastern and the Great Central had both built 4-6-0s for mixed traffic work. The most modern of these were the Raven 'B16s', 70 of which were built in 1919-24, and the 38 Robinson 'B7s' of 1921-24. The 'B16s' had the same cylinder dimensions, coupled wheel diameter and boiler pressure as the 'K3s', but the heating surface was much less. Gresley thought that the class could bear investment in improvements, and Stamer, and later Thompson, whilst Mechanical Engineer at Darlington, provided boilers with greater heating surface; moreover in 1936 Gresley initiated a thoroughgoing modernisation of selected members of the class, in which Walschaerts valve gear, longer travel valves, and derived motion for the inside valve replaced the original three sets of Stephenson gear, effecting a substantial improvement in performance. The seven rebuilds, of which No 2364 was the first, were classified 'B16/2'. After Thompson became CME he resumed rebuilding the 'B16s', but with his own preference for three separate sets of Walschaerts valve gear; commencing with No 922, 17 were rebuilt in this way from 1944 to 1949, Class B16/3. Both the rebuilds exhibited clear Gresley lineaments in the high side window cabs and raised, curving running plate, but strangely the Darlington chimney was continued, complete with capuchon. It is perhaps surprising too that Thompson did not provide the 'B16/3s' with his standard boiler, a variant of that originally fitted to the 'B17s', and later applied to the 'B1s' and other rebuilds, but it is understood that there would have been difficulty in accommodating the firebox within the frames. He did however contemplate rebuilding the 'B7s' with the 'B1'-type boiler and replacing the four cylinders by his two standard 20in×26in, but this was not proceeded with.

Another rebuild which did take place was of 'K3' No 206, in which the 6ft diameter boiler was retained, but pressed to 225lb/sq in, and the three cylinders replaced by two outside cylinders 20in×26in, giving a tractive effort only a little less than that of the 'K3'. The conversion, which took place in 1945, was given the classification 'K5', and in comparative tests on the road against a standard K3, a small saving in fuel was noted, but evidently not sufficient to warrant any further rebuilding of the class, as No 206 remained a one-off. A factor probably ignored in the conversion was the effect on the frames of the heavier thrust of the two, larger, cylinders.

The locomotive class for which Edward Thompson will be best remembered is undoubtedly his general service 4-6-0, the 'B1'. This was the type of locomotive the LNER were to need in quantity in the later 1940s and whether or not the need could have been met by the 'V4', Thompson saw a radically different solution: build a 2-cylinder 4-6-0 'entirely composed of standard parts which would be roughly equivalent to the existing 'K3' engines but of simpler design'. That was what he put to his Board on 13 July 1942, when approval was given for the construction of 10 of this new class at a cost of £8,050 each. This was the 'B1' class, the first of which, then numbered 8301 and named *Springbok* was completed at Darlington in December 1942. Despite his assurance to his Directors, Thompson did not build the locomotive entirely from standard parts. This could hardly have been the case anyway, as at least a new design of frames would have been required, but he did his best. The boiler was that used for the 'B17', strengthened to withstand a working pressure of 225lb/sq in. The 20in×26in cylinders were similar to those of the 'K2', but new patterns had to be made as the slide bar arrangements were of the 3-bar type. Tractive effort was 26,878lb, over 3,000lb less than that of the 'K3'. The wheels, rods and motion were similar to those of the 'V2', but the bogie design was changed from the later Gresley pattern, although retaining the side control springs. One important factor was a reduction in the balancing of the reciprocating parts, which reduced the hammer blow of this 2-cylinder locomotive to no more than that of the 3-cylinder 'B17'. This was no doubt a concession to the Civil Engineer in order to obtain as wide a route availability as possible, the maximum axle load in any case being less than 18 tons, but it was at the expense of a smooth ride; the 'B1s' were not noted for comfort, especially in run down condition.

The class rightly obtained a very favourable reception. The LNER operating authorities welcomed the 'B1' as a type of locomotive which they badly needed, although they had to wait several years before it became available in quantity. It was a straightforward design and relatively easy to maintain, without the complications of the '2 to 1' gear. And, to a railway press which had recently seen the Bulleid Class Q1 0-6-0 as an example of a locomotive built under wartime conditions, the classic outline of the 'B1' was a revelation. Indeed at first glance it could easily have been a Gresley design, provided of course that Sir Nigel had been converted to 2-cylinder operation. Closer inspection however revealed subtle changes in the line of the footplating — higher and straighter than Gresley would have adopted, with a reversion to the Darlington quadrants in place of the gentler 'S' curve. To the purist, the profile was spoiled by the short cab sides, which were cut off several inches above the line of the tender footplating. Thompson might well have argued the additional metal was unnecessary, and to omit it saved a few pounds weight per engine, or several tons in aggregate when the class was built in quantity. Anyway, the Gresley round topped firebox was retained, as were his boiler mountings, cab and smokebox; had Thompson so wished, he could have changed a great deal more.

So, Thompson's first essay into locomotive design was given approbation from all sides: a worthy successor to Gresley, observers considered. This however was not a view shared by all on the CME's staff, who had suffered from Thompson's managerial vagaries — but that is another story. For a few brief weeks all appeared well to the outsider, but in January 1943 the first rebuilt 'P2' appeared, and commentators wondered if it was the product of the same man.

The 'B1' was of course intended eventually to replace all the variegated pre-grouping 4-4-0s, 4-4-2s and 4-6-0s, as well as taking over the faster passenger duties which fell to 0-6-0s such as the 'J39'. Construction began slowly; the second example did not appear until June 1943, and it took another year before the initial batch of 10 were completed. In fact, only 25 in all had been delivered by the time Thompson retired, but he had laid the foundations for a large fleet.

In April 1945 he put his five year postwar building programme to the Board, under which 1,000 locomotives were to be withdrawn and replaced by a like number of new or rebuilt engines, including 400 of his new 4-6-0s. And, despite nationalisation on 1 January 1948, 400 were in fact built. Forty more came from Darlington in 1946/7, no fewer than 290 from the North British Loco Co (the last in 1952), 50 from the Vulcan Foundry, 10 from Gorton, and two final batches from Darlington, all of which, with the initial 10, took the BR numbers from 61000 to 61409. Originally they were referred to simply as the 'B' class, semi-officially as the 'Antelopes', as the first batches were named after species of this animal, and unofficially as 'Bongos', one unfortunate locomotive bearing the name of this beast. They penetrated virtually every part of the system, from Kings Cross to the Great North of Scotland, where they were the first new locomotives for over a quarter of a century. The big Thompson and Peppercorn 6ft 2in Pacifics were regarded as mixed traffic engines, but the 'B1s' were the final LNER design in the true mixed traffic sense, able to cope with anything from a pickup goods to the emergency relief of a failed Pacific.

A question never to be answered is: 'Given the circumstances, would Gresley have produced a "B1"?' Well, the answer could be that he might well have done so, but he would never have rebuilt *Cock o' the North*.

Chapter 6

Freight Locomotives

Not only did the Great Northern enjoy a substantial business in transporting coal, the main source of energy for heating in those days, but there was also a good deal of other slow moving freight and mineral traffic. Until the decline in coal movement in the 1920s, most of this traffic was continued by the LNER, whilst the sugar beet industry, centred in Lincolnshire, provided a new, although seasonal, source of revenue. Nigel Gresley reckoned that he had solved the question of the GNR need for powerful mixed traffic locomotives by the introduction of his 2-cylinder 2-6-0s and saw no reason, apart from minor improvements, to alter Ivatt's superheated 5ft 2in 0-6-0, later LNER Class J6, to meet the continuing need for new locomotives for short distance and pick-up goods work, and which also possessed the ability to help out on passenger work when necessary. But Ivatt's 'Long Tom' 0-8-0s were insufficient in number for all the GNR long haul mineral workings, from the South Yorkshire and Nottingham pits to the yards at New England, Peterborough, and thence to the railhead at Ferme Park, Hornsey. On this route the long loose-coupled hauls occupied the same tracks as faster trains on those sections of the GNR which did not possess relief lines, suffering delays to themselves whilst waiting for block sections to be cleared and obstructing following passenger trains as they dragged their loads slowly along. It was evident that more heavy freight locomotives were needed: Gresley reasoned that he could improve substantially on the 'Long Toms', and this he did with an imposing 2-8-0 design, the first of which appeared in December 1913, enabling the main line coal trains to be increased from 60 to 80 wagons. These engines had two large 21in×28in cylinders supplied with steam from a 5ft 6in diameter superheated boiler with 2,492sq ft of heating surface; this class introduced outside steam pipes, a later easily recognisable Gresley feature. Four more were built at Doncaster in 1914, and a further 15 came from the North British Locomotive Company in 1919; all were numbered in sequence after the 0-8-0s, taking the GNR numbers 456-460 and 462-476.

In between these two batches, however, a most important locomotive development took place, when in May 1918 a new version of the 2-8-0 type was completed at Doncaster, GNR No 461, generally similar to the original 2-cylinder class, but with three 18in×26in cylinders, 3-bar pattern slidebars, and of the greatest interest to locomotive engineers, Gresley's conjugated valvegear, by which the drive for the valve gear of the inside cylinder was derived from the outside Walschaerts motion. However the arrangement, which had been patented by Gresley, was unnecessarily complex, and a further apparent disadvantage was that all three cylinders were steeply inclined. When later batches were constructed, a revised design of conjugated gear was adopted, incorporating improvements suggested by Holcroft. This class, LNER '02', was effectively Gresley's standard heavy freight locomotive, and more were constructed in GNR and early LNER days to take the numbers up to 3501. However the class was not to be built in great quantity because of the availability of other classes of 2-8-0 constructed to Government orders during the two world wars, and only three other batches were built — Nos 2954-61 in 1932, Nos 2430-37 in 1933/4, and Nos 3833-57 in 1942/3. These were provided with LNER side window cabs, an improvement on the GNR cutaway type fitted to the earlier examples. Perhaps Gresley had a fondness for his original 2-8-0, No 3461, as it was never rebuilt to conform to the later style of valve gear.

Unlike his large passenger engines, Gresley's 2-8-0s were not normally seen outside the Great Northern section, or the March to Temple Mills, Stratford, line. The heaviest mineral haulage in the North Eastern Area remained the prerogative of the native 0-8-0s, whilst Robinson 2-8-0s ran the Great Central freight trains, as well as operating in Lincolnshire, from Hull, and into Aberdeen from the South. Other regional trains, often very heavy, continued to be hauled by the large 0-6-0s of the Great Eastern and North British, as they had been before the grouping. The situation was of course radically altered during and after World War 2, when Stanier and later the 'Austerity' 2-8-0s were available in quantity, the latter penetrating to virtually all parts of the system.

When, in early LNER days, locomotive building programmes were being formulated, it became clear that no new heavy freight locomotives need be built for some years, as there were large quantities of Robinson's Great Central 2-8-0. LNER Class 04, available from Government disposal agencies, 518 of these engines having been built late in World War 1 and afterwards for service overseas or for continuation of employment during the rundown from munitions work. To add to the Great Central stock, already totalling 148 at grouping (including 18 with a larger diameter boiler, classed '05', subsequently rebuilt to the standard '04'), a further 125 were purchased in 1923 for £2,000 each. 48 more followed in 1925, at £1,500 each, and a final 100 in 1927, by which time the price had fallen to £340, little more than scrap value. All had been used for a time on loan to other railways, and all required renovation, but as part of a package the LNER also acquired quantities of parts at knockdown prices. As the years went by, Gresley rebuilt some of the '04s' by replacing the Robinson boiler by his own type with round topped firebox, as fitted to the '02s', and all continued at work until 1941, when 92 were sent to the Middle East, where on some duties they worked alongside newly built Stanier 2-8-0s of LMS Class 8F. The simplicity and ruggedness of the Robinson design appealed to their wartime operators, who claimed that they shrugged off the disadvantages of working in desert conditions, including lubrication by what was effectively a mixture of oil and sand. The LNER was required to put the '04s' in good order before despatching them overseas, the boilers to be good for at least two years. For some it was their second trip abroad, having been in France at the end of World War 1. The price eventually negotiated in 1947 brought the LNER £5,700 per engine. It has been said that when the first suggestions were made in 1939 that a large number of '04s' were to be requisitioned, Gresley offered the entire class in exchange for materials to construct an equivalent number of his own '02s'. This, if true, could only have been put up as a bargaining point, as the LNER could not have afforded to have given up such a large tranche of its locomotive stock and still have maintained the growing wartime freight movement.

Although after the grouping there was no real need for the construction of new heavy freight locomotives, Gresley was not content to rest with the 2-8-0 type, and obtained authority to build two larger engines. Since the Pennsylvania 'K4s' Pacific had a freight counterpart in a 2-8-2 design, Class L1s, it was a natural desire on Gresley's part, once he had proved his own Pacific, to develop a Mikado of his own, and two were turned out from Doncaster in 1925, 2393/94, Class P1, with boiler and cylinder dimensions the same as those of the original 'A1' Pacifics. 5ft 2in coupled wheels were intended to give the class a higher turn of speed than the '02s', whilst their tractive effort was a respectable 38,500lb, increased to some 47,000lb by the use of a booster engine powering the trailing wheels. The booster was evidently an afterthought, and whilst well intentioned, to assist in starting, and hauling trains up the long 1 in 200 banks of the Great Northern main line, it was not successful in practice. The traffic objective of the 'P1s' was to enable the Ferme Park coal hauls to be increased to 100 wagons, a 25% increase on the trailing load permitted for the '02s'; it was also envisaged that the Mikados would be used on the Wath to Immingham run as well, but this was not to be the case. However, whilst very long freight trains were the vogue in the United States, these were fitted with continuous brakes, and could be moved as a single unit, unlike the cumbersome trains of individual loose-coupled 4-wheeled wagons of contemporary British practice. The 'P1s' demonstrated Gresley's point that he could produce engines which could cope with 100 wagon trains, but unfortunately the Operating Department were unable to handle such loads, as the trains were too long for operating convenience, sometimes overlapping three block sections, whilst coupling breakage was an ever-present hazard. Although well-proportioned and good looking locomotives — Bulleid is quoted as saying he thought they were one of Gresley's best — operating difficulties led to a predictably early demise, and they were the first of Gresley's engines to be deliberately withdrawn, in 1945. Prior to withdrawal, in 1942/3 they had received 'A3'-type 220lb boilers, and like 'A1s' rebuilt as 'A3s' had their cylinders reduced to 19in diameter.

Ivatt's 0-6-0 had been quietly multiplied on the Great Northern by Gresley until the last batch was constructed in 1922, when 110 were in service. However, despite its universal popularity as a maid-of-all-work on almost every railway in Britain, the 0-6-0 type suffered a fundamental defect in that its lack of guiding wheels gave rise to excessive wear on the flanges and axleboxes of the leading coupled wheels. Gresley, appreciating the problem, sought in 1924 to improve on the 0-6-0 by introducing a 5ft 2in 2-6-0. But instead of designing a cheaper, lower powered locomotive, his proposal was for a 3-cylinder engine with 18in×26in cylinders, which would have proved appreciably more expensive than an 0-6-0. In consequence, the proposal made no headway.

However, the LNER needed further 0-6-0s to replace older locomotives due for withdrawal, and a standard design was worked up at Darlington, for use on all sections of the system except those with severe weight limitations. One might have

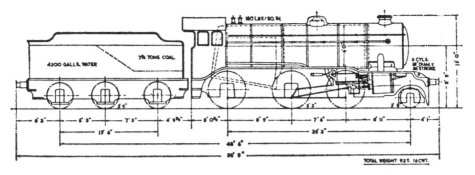

Drawing of proposed 5ft 2in 2-6-0, 1924

thought that an updated version of the Great Northern 'J6' would have been chosen for this, but the immediate post-grouping need was not on the Great Northern, but elsewhere, and the decision was taken to design a more powerful class, equivalent in power to the North Eastern 'J27', a Worsdell design of 1906, which Raven had continued to build up to 1923. The first 35 were turned out from Darlington in 1926, with 4ft 8in coupled wheels, and were specifically intended to work coal traffic from the Fife coal fields. These were classed 'J38', and occupied vacant numbers in the North Eastern series between Nos 1400 and 1447. No others were built with this wheel dimension, as, with the objective of allowing them to be used when required on secondary passenger and excursion trains, all subsequent examples had 5ft 2in coupled wheels. 289 in all were built down to 1941, Class J39, all at Darlington except for 28 which came from Beyer Peacock in 1936/7. The first 'J39' followed the 'J38' sequence by bearing the number 1448, and later construction filled other vacant numbers in the North Eastern series, particularly when the locomotives in question were allocated to North Eastern sheds, whilst others were numbered in blocks in the later post-grouping series. The final batch took Nos 3081-3098, Great Northern numbers which had been vacant for many years.

The 'J38/J39' was a new design, not a Gresley implant on the traditional North Eastern style of 0-6-0, although the Darlington influence could be discerned in the smokebox door and other details, and, whilst the running plate was raised in the Gresley fashion, it had Darlington quadrants rather than the double curve of Doncaster. The cab was LNER, and a newly designed boiler was fitted, originally 6in longer on the 'J38s' than on the 'J39s' and also to be adapted the following year to the 'D49s'; the inside valve gear was derived from the Robinson 'A5' 4-6-2Ts. The flexibility of the 'J39s' was welcomed by the Operating Department, particularly in the North Eastern Area, but in the final days of steam when all that remained for 0-6-0s was short haul mineral trains, the more solid 'J27s' outlasted the 'J39s'.

With Gresley's authority, Thompson whilst Mechanical Engineer at Stratford, had begun to rebuild the 'Claud Hamilton' 4-4-0s with round topped fireboxes and new boilers, and from 1934 this improvement was applied to the Great Eastern 'J18' and 'J19' 0-6-0s. Later, as CME, he began to rebuild the large 'J20s' with the round topped firebox and boiler designed for the rebuilt 'B12/4' 4-6-0s, and all eventually were converted, the later rebuilds taking their boilers from scrapped

4-6-0s. All these conversions exhibited the typical smooth Gresley profile. A further proposal, but this time not put into effect, was for a rebuild of the small North Eastern 'J21' 0-6-0 with a new boiler pressed to 200lb/sq in, and new frames, cylinders and valves, and intended for the Stainmore line. The specification was at pains to point out that the existing tender was to be retained, but little of the original locomotive would have remained.

In Great Northern days, Gresley had initiated some improvement in the Ivatt 0-6-0 and 0-8-0 classes by fitting many of these with new boilers, and he later followed this by applying the boiler from his own 2-8-0s to a number of the Robinson '04s'. However after Thompson had assumed office, he introduced a major reconstruction of the '04' in which little more than the original frame remained. With a 225lb/sq in boiler and his standard 20in×26in cylinders, the rebuilds, classed '01', rated a tractive effort of 35,518lb, and were regarded as amongst his more successful locomotives. By the time the programme ceased in October 1949, 58 had been converted. An even more widespread conversion was the fitting of his standard boiler to the '04s' but retaining the existing cylinders and motion. No fewer than 98 '04s' were so altered, to utilise a standard component and avoid construction of further Robinson boilers. The first conversion came out in 1944, but most were completed under British Railways in the 1950s.

Thompson also rebuilt a Gresley 'K4' 2-6-0 with a shorter version of his 225lb boiler, but retaining the 20in×26in cylinders. Reclassified 'K1', under Peppercorn a further 70 examples were built after nationalisation. However, as in earlier years when Robinson 2-8-0s had been purchased from Government surplus sources, history was repeated after the second world war when 200 'Austerity' 2-8-0s (LNER Class 07) were similarly acquired, once again avoiding the need for large scale construction of new freight locomotives. These however could not be said to owe very much to Gresley's design principles.

Thompson also visualised the need for a third, smaller, freight class, with the potential to be pressed into passenger service if necessary, and selected another Great Central class, the 'J11' 0-6-0 dating from 1901, for modernisation, but in a much less radical manner than with the '04s'. The non-standard boiler with its

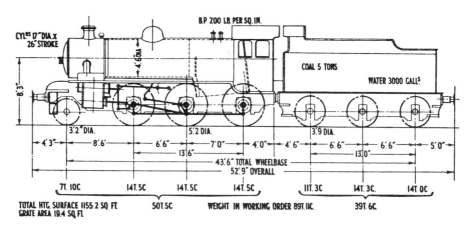

Drawing of proposed 'K6' lightweight 2-6-0, 1947.

Belpaire firebox and GC cutaway cab remained but new cylinders with long travel piston valves were provided, thus necessitating raising the pitch of the boiler, which in turn led to a shorter chimney. This apart, little outward change was evident. As with all Gorton products, the 'J11' was a rugged engine, and despite its age still possessed the capability for many years good running. Presumably it was this factor which decided Thompson to preserve the class, rather than the 'J39' or even the 'J6'. He was not wholly anti-GNR, as he proposed to adopt the 'J50' as his medium shunting tank, and the 'J6' would have made an appropriate stable mate if Edwardian designs were to be perpetuated. But the 'J11' conversion remained pure Robinson in appearance and far removed from any outward influence of Gresley.

As a final still-born proposal, a small 2-6-0 with an axle load below 15tons was projected in 1947 for freight and passenger work on lightly laid branch lines; this, tentatively classed 'K6', and the last locomotive to be delineated under LNER auspices, introduced the novelty of a half-cab on the tender, and although with only two cylinders, clearly maintained the Gresley style of outline.

Chapter 7

Passenger Tank Locomotives and Railcars

The main Great Northern services which called for operation by tank engines were the inner suburban workings from Kings Cross and Moorgate to Hatfield, together with the associated branch lines, and the West Riding local trains based on Leeds and Bradford. Locomotives had increased in size and capability from 0-4-2T to 0-4-4T under Stirling, and 4-4-2T to 0-6-2T under Ivatt (with a short period during which a number of 0-8-2Ts were employed). The last 25 of Ivatt's 0-6-2Ts were built at Doncaster in 1911/12, after Gresley had taken over, but these had been authorised during Ivatt's last year as Locomotive Engineer, and Gresley did nothing to alter the design.

Although end-to-end runs were relatively short — Kings Cross to Hatfield is only 17.7 miles — smart timings were characteristic of the services, and quite fast running took place between stations. The Ivatt 0-6-2Ts, LNER Class N1, supplemented by a number of the somewhat underpowered 'C12' 4-4-2Ts, dealt adequately with the London suburban traffic until at the end of World War 1 an urgent need arose for more powerful passenger tank locomotives, not because of shortcomings on the part of the 'N1s', but because there were not enough of them to cope with growing loads and traffic. It had been the GNR practice to build new locomotives for the London suburban lines, and use the displaced engines in the provinces, and this process was repeated by Gresley. New locomotives were built for the London end of the system, and the 'C12s' were transferred away, in their turn displacing Stirling 0-4-4Ts which were then withdrawn. Despite the absence of guiding wheels, and consequent high degree of wear on the flanges of the front coupled wheels, the 'N1s' were fair riders and had a good turn of speed, particularly downhill into London with the trailing wheels leading. Gresley saw no reason why this wheel arrangement should not be perpetuated, and with an updated version of the 0-6-2T in mind had experimented with Ivatt's design by superheating one for trial purposes; later another 10 received superheaters.

In considering a new locomotive for the London inner suburban trains, Gresley was severely constrained by the impossibility of lengthening the platform roads at Moorgate terminus, and by the need to pack in as many commuters into the trains as possible. Employing his system of articulation, he had evolved an eight coach train consisting of two four-coach sets, known as 'Quad-arts', which could hold 632 passengers in three classes, and almost as many standing. An 'N1' and a quad-art train neatly fitted into the Moorgate platform roads, and nothing longer could be contemplated. So the 'N2' was designed, and despite its much more modern appearance — a true Gresley outline in fact, contrasted with the severity of the Ivatt outline of its predecessor — it was essentially the 'N1' updated with larger tanks, piston valves and Gresley's own patent double header superheater. The piston valves required the boiler to be pitched higher, and consequently the chimney was shorter, but the boiler remained the same, apart from the addition of the superheater and the consequent rearrangement of tubes and flues. Cylinders were enlarged from 18in×26in to 19in×26in. Sixty were ordered at once, virtually straight off the drawing board, which indicated the fullest confidence in their capability. Nor was this to be misplaced, as the 'N2s' and their quad-art companions provided the backbone of the GN Section suburban services for the next 40 years. The first GNR 10 (LNER Nos 4606-15) were built at Doncaster and 50 came from the North British Loco Co (Nos 4721-70), all in 1920/21, and until repainted by the LNER all were in green livery. Later batches were built mainly by contractors up to 1929, including a number sent to Scotland, originally to meet a request made at the grouping by the North British Operating Department for a further 10 Reid 4-4-2Ts. Altogether 107 'N2s' were built, several also working in the West Riding, and assisting with empty carriage movements at Kings Cross. The LNER built examples were numbered 892-7, 2583-94 and 2662-90.

Both Ivatt and Gresley had considered a longer wheelbase tank engine, and Ivatt had introduced his 0-8-2T in 1903, when the 'C12' was the current standard class of GNR suburban tank, but this was too long for many of the curves, and too heavy for much of the track in the vicinity of Kings Cross, and soon gravitated elsewhere on the system. He had also considered an inside-cylindered 2-6-2T at the same time as the 'N1', but this was not taken further. Gresley's first 2-6-2T design was proposed at the same time as the 'K3', and would have had the same cylinders and coupled wheel diameter, although with a smaller boiler of 5ft 6in in diameter. Over 4ft longer than the 'N1', it would have been forbidden to work to Moorgate. After further consideration, to operate outer suburban services from Kings Cross, perhaps even to Cambridge, the design was elongated to a 2-6-4T, and this was proposed once more, in 1925, with some detail updating, including a side window cab. But the newly built Pacifics had released sufficient Atlantics and 4-4-0s for such duties, and so long as these had plenty of running in them, there was no merit in introducing a new class which could not work turn about with the 'N2s' into Moorgate.

Apart from the GNR suburban services, at grouping Gresley and the LNER were presented with the responsibility for other short distance services, and many of these needed new locomotives. An exception was the Great Central system out of Marylebone, but this was not very extensive and in any case in 1911 Robinson had introduced an excellent class of 4-6-2T to this work, a further 10 of which had been built in 1923 to a GC pregrouping order. Around Newcastle upon Tyne the North Eastern 'G5s' had a fair life remaining, although outclassed on the hardest turns, whilst the 'H1' 4-4-4Ts covered many of the longer distance services, not always with the greatest efficiency, due to the inherent liability to wheelslip of this type. So, to provide additional power on Tyneside and Tees-side, Gresley decided that rather than perpetuate an unsatisfactory design he would build a further batch of the only really capable large passenger tank engines on the LNER, the

Robinson 4-6-2T, LNER Class A5. Thirteen were constructed by Hawthorn Leslie in 1925/6 and were given vacant numbers in the 1700s. Later, in 1931-36, originally at the instigation of A. C. Stamer, the 'H1s' were rebuilt into 4-6-2Ts, and reclassified 'A8', following which they gained a new lease of life and widened their sphere of operation. However neither the well proportioned 'A5s' — which retained the Belpaire boiler — nor the 'A8s' with their massive side tanks and outside cylinders with inside steam chests and valve gear could be said in any way to have resembled a Gresley product. Each bore the stamp of its respective pre-grouping designer.

An urgent need both for locomotives and coaching stock for suburban services was diagnosed at the outset on the Great Eastern. A. J. Hill had introduced a class of 0-6-2T for this work, but completely different from the 'N2' in that it possessed a smaller boiler with Belpaire firebox, 18in×24in cylinders and 4ft 10in coupled wheels, intended for rapid acceleration from stations only short distances apart. Wisely, Gresley saw that this was not a job for the 'N2' (although a few were drafted in for a time on longer GE outer suburban hauls) and put in hand further batches of the local product, LNER Class N7, together with articulated train sets broadly similar to those on the Great Northern, but with five coaches per set and known as 'quint-arts'. Including 22 built before the grouping, 134 'N7s' were constructed by 1928, the last 32 coming from Doncaster; strangely exactly twice as many of the Great Eastern 'N7s' were built there as of the native design, the 'N2'. Other batches of 'N7s' came from Gorton, Beardmore, and Robert Stephenson. The Doncaster series had round topped fireboxes and GN pattern smokebox doors, but the 'N7s' retained their typical Stratford lineaments and there was little about them, even with the Doncaster refinements, to suggest any Gresley influence. Although the 'N7s' did not migrate as far as the 'N2s', they were tried from time on Great Central services, and in the West Riding, whilst for several years a number worked on the Great Northern, taking turns with the 'N2s' from Kings Cross, but particularly working the branch lines from Hatfield and Welwyn Garden City. Like the 'N2s', the first batches of which were numbered in the Great Northern series, the 'N7s' ordered before the grouping naturally bore numbers in the Great Eastern series, but those built for the LNER received lower numbers. The longest consecutive run of 'N7s' was Nos 2600-61, whilst other

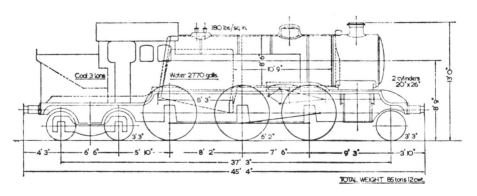

Drawing of proposed Stratford design of 6ft 2in 2-6-4T, 1927.

batches filled gaps in the 400s, 800s and 900s in place of withdrawn North Eastern engines. It is interesting to note that in his preliminary survey of LNER locomotive classes, Thompson considered the 'N7' as a class to be maintained. Possibly he had a liking for these compact engines, powerful for their size, which he had improved by redesigning the valve arrangements during his time at Stratford.

Gresley made another attempt to introduce a larger passenger tank locomotive in 1927 when a 2-6-4T with 6ft 2in wheels was outlined at Stratford, particularly to meet the requirements of Southend line services. However the Operating Department were less than keen on the introduction of a new design of limited range and capacity when the Great Eastern system as a whole was crying out for more and larger locomotives. They repeated their request for additional 4-6-0s' and in response got another 10 'B12s', and eventually the 'B17s'.

However, elsewhere on the system, the need was growing for a new, larger, passenger tank engine class, and in 1930 Gresley's long awaited 2-6-2T at last emerged. This was the 'V1' which with its derivative the 'V3' was the only class in which his 3-cylinder system and conjugated valve gear were actually built into a tank locomotive, apart from the Worsborough banker, although there had been several other proposals. The 'V1' design went through a number of modifications before finality was reached, its designer eventually achieving a well-proportioned layout with a 5ft diameter boiler having 1,609sq ft heating surface 180lb/sq in pressure, 16in×26in cylinders, 5ft 8in coupled wheels, and a double side window cab. Mainly employed in Scotland and the north-east, and later on the Great Eastern, 92 were built between 1930 and 1940, all at Doncaster. The last 10 had boilers pressed to 200lb/sq in, and during the 1950s, as boilers required renewal, replacements were to be to the new standard, involving reclassification to 'V3'. At first numbered consecutively from 2900-33, later deliveries took numbers in the 300s and 400s, apart from three which became 2897-9. As with the 'D49s', when new, one of the first batch No 2911, had a short period of trial from Kings Cross. The 'V1/V3' created a favourable impression from both performance and appearance aspects, particularly the later examples which had a hopper type of coal bunker; had circumstances been normal, more would have been built, but later orders were cancelled during the war. One shortcoming however was their limited water capacity which tended to restrict their activities; they could not be used on the Southend services, for example. Years later, in 1946, a proposal was considered for rebuilding with substantially larger tanks, and Thompson's 225lb/sq in boiler and 20in×26in cylinders, but this was not proceeded with.

At the time the 'V4' 2-6-2 was being developed, Gresley took yet another look at a large tank locomotive, and drawings were prepared for a 2-6-4T with 'V4' cylinders and coupled wheels, a rather smaller tapered boiler, and, unusually for a tank engine, a wide firebox. An alternative with two cylinders was also considered, whilst a third drawing, of a 4-6-2T wheel arrangement, with 5ft 2in driving wheels, was firmly marked 'No' in Gresley's blue pencil.

When Edward Thompson had finally decided on his plans for new and rebuilt locomotives to form the future LNER standard classes, he circulated particulars of these in a booklet to the LNER directors. This included photographs of the engines in question, all of which had appeared by that time, at least in prototype, except his proposed 2-6-4T. Nevertheless a photograph was included purporting to be of one of this class, but in fact it was no more than a doctored picture of a 'V1' to which a trailing bogie and a longer side tank had been added in the photographer's laboratory. When his locomotive eventually appeared, classified 'L1', it proved to be a powerful machine with a tractive effort of 32,080lb. The boiler was very similar to that of the 'V1', but pressed to 225lb/sq in, the cylinders were Thompson's standard 20in×26in, and the coupled wheels were 5ft 2in diameter. He had evidently concluded that such small wheels would aid acceleration, whilst good front end design would permit high speeds. Perhaps he should have taken more note of the shortcomings of the 'K4s' on the Clydeside portion of the West Highland line before committing himself to such a small wheel diameter. Anyway, although the 'L1' could put up a surprising turn of speed, this was at the expense of the mechanism; the locomotive was in fact too powerful for its structure, and axleboxes, cylinders and even smokebox saddles worked loose, whilst tank leakage also posed a problem. At the other end of the speed spectrum, it had been thought that the 'L1' would have proved useful on short but heavy mineral hauls, but trials soon indicated what surely ought to have been already known, that the tank engine's braking power was insufficient to control this type of train with safety. However 100 were built between 1945 and 1950, and the class operated outer suburban services from Kings Cross with fair success, sharing the work with the 'B1s' as by that time all the GN 4-4-0s and Atlantics had gone. They also worked from Hull, and replaced the 'A5s' on the Marylebone services, and 'V1s' on the Great Eastern, on which section they seemed most at home. But their conception was clearly that of Thompson, and they lacked the elegance of the 'V1'.

Many railways, both before and after the grouping, operated branch line services on the 'pull-and-push' system, with a small tank engine and a coach or two, often increased at busy periods if the engine could manage the additional load. To reduce the operating costs of such services, in 1904 the GNR purchased a petrol driven rail car, but this was not a success, and soon afterwards six steam rail cars were obtained, two each from the Avonside Engine Company, Kitson & Co, and Doncaster. Each consisted of a diminutive 0-4-0T and a bogie coach, mounted on a single frame. They lasted into the 1920s.

Gresley however did not follow this practice, and when after the formation of the LNER a clear need was identified for something less costly than the typcial push-and-pull set for many branch lines, a number of steam rail cars were purchased powered by a small 2-cylinder engine, similar to those in the Sentinel shunting engines. These cars were not wholly reliable, and had little capability for sustained overload, but despite criticism at many levels, more were bought. These included a number built by the Clayton Wagon Co and others of improved Sentinel designs including many with a 6-cylinder 100hp engine; there were also five with twin 6-cylinder engines, and one in which two units were articulated together. Altogether 92 steam rail cars were purchased, and whilst operating costs were said to have been half those of a push-and-pull auto-train, the light construction of the railcars and their unreliability meant a lifespan of only 10 to 15 years. However their attractive green and cream livery gave them a cheerful appearance compared with the grimy brown of the usual branch line coach, and in contrast to the usual anonymity of such stock, almost all the steam railcars bore the names of old time stage coaches.

In 1934, three 250hp diesel-electric railcars were purchased from Armstrong Whitworth, not for branch line service, but for shorter distance main line services in the north-east; there was also a smaller, lightweight, diesel railcar with a 95hp engine. These pioneer vehicles gave a great deal of trouble and were withdrawn after a few years' service. In a further experiment, a railcar made by Ganz of Hungary was tried in 1939 in the Selby and Pontefract area. After trials in the Newcastle locality in 1944 of GWR diesel-mechanical railcar No 19, the idea was revived in the early postwar years, the North Eastern Area Operating Department calculating that 57 railcars and 7 trailers would save £105,000 a year on running costs. However the proposal did not reach the Board, and with impending nationalisation the matter was dropped.

The diesel engine is much more suited to the railcar concept than was the steam engine, but it is interesting to observe Gresley's efforts in persisting with the Sentinels because he believed that they were tailored to the job. For the same reason, he tried the diesel-electric railcar, before the Great Western introduced their diesel-mechanical version.

Chapter 8

Freight Tank Locomotives

Early in the development of the steam locomotive it was realised that for certain applications there was no point in providing a separate vehicle to carry coal and water — particularly if the range of operation was limited, or if there was frequent reversal of direction, as when shunting. For these purposes, designs evolved in which coal was carried in a bunker behind the cab, and water in tanks beside the boiler or in a well between the frames. Now, one of the fascinations of the study of the steam locomotive is the apparent inconsequence of designers who produced different solutions to essentially the same problem. One would have thought that after a century of development certain best practices would have emerged in most aspects of design. This certainly occurred in many important areas, but one point was never finally settled: where in a locomotive intended for shunting goods wagons should the water be carried? Almost to the end of the development of the conventional steam locomotive, there were three schools of thought. Some practitioners opted for the usual side tanks, others for a tank in the form of a saddle over the boiler, whilst Swindon opinion favoured tanks shaped like panniers, slung on each side of the boiler.

Many early designers featured a fourth alternative in the well tank, but the limited storage capacity of this soon led designers to seek other methods. On the Great Northern, Patrick Stirling preferred the saddle tank, in which the water was carried in a semi-circular tank around the boiler, stopping short of the footplating to allow space for access beneath the boiler. Drawbacks of this type of tank were the need to pierce it to provide for the boiler mountings, whilst particularly when worn, injector trouble could be caused by water in the saddle tank becoming warmed by the boiler. The saddle tank was a particular favourite for small shunting tank engines used in industry, but was not used widely by other railways, nowhere receiving such lasting acceptance as on the Great Northern. Stirling neatly avoided two-thirds of the boiler mounting problem by ending the tank short of the smokebox, so leaving this clear for the chimney, and of course omitting the steam dome. Ivatt continued the tradition, although adding a dome, but Gresley chose to introduce side tanks, extending to the front of the smokebox, but with sloping tops to aid visibility when buffering up, and substantial apertures to permit access to the motion. Concurrently, most other railways, and especially the Midland and later the LMS with their neat 'Jinty', favoured a shorter side tank, whilst the Great Western, so often contrary, persisted with a pannier design.

After construction of a number of smaller engines of a similar type, Stirling's standard saddle tank first emerged in 1874, and was built in successive batches during his regime and that of Ivatt with only minor dimensional increases; by 1909 over 250 had been built. Gresley's side tank version first appeared in 1913, and a revision, with a slightly larger boiler, LNER Class J50, in 1922. In course of time the earlier Gresley examples were reboilered and eventually the class totalled 102. Over the years between 1874 and 1939, when the last 'J50' was turned into traffic, the main dimensions of this essentially GNR design increased from $17\frac{1}{2}$in × 26in cylinders to $18\frac{1}{2}$in × 26in, heating surface from 857 to 1,119sq ft, and boiler pressure from 160 to 170lb/sq in. As a result, tractive effort went up from 19,334lb to 22,963lb, but probably one of the most useful results of the change from saddle to side tank was the increase in water capacity from 960 to 1,520 gallons. All the 'J50s' were built at Doncaster, except the last 14, which came from Gorton. Originally numbered in the GN series, later batches took vacant numbers in the 500s, 600s, and 1000s, as well as Nos 2789-94 in the post-grouping series. Most of the class spent their time in the West Riding, a few going to Eastfield, Glasgow, to Immingham, and to Stratford. Some penetrated other parts of the system for short periods, but not until after nationalisation were they to be found at New England or Ferme Park, which remained the haunts of the saddle tanks until old age forced their withdrawal in the 1950s.

Although the 'J50' was essentially a Gresley revision of the Stirling/Ivatt saddle tank it replaced, and despite the substitution of the side tanks for the saddle tank, the outline of the locomotive smacked more of Ivatt than of Gresley: perhaps it was the tall chimney and dome, but the appearance was certainly Edwardian.

None of the other LNER constituents possessed an 0-6-0T as powerful as the 'J50', and indeed the Great Central, the North British and the North Eastern favoured the 0-6-2T for much of their yard shunting and trip work. The North British 'N15' was equivalent to the 'J50' in power, but the others were smaller and older. The 'N15' was an exception to Whitelaw's policy (whilst Chairman of the North British) of not placing orders for new locomotives during the years immediately preceding the grouping, as, leaving the LNER to pick up the bill, 30 were built in 1923/4, the final batch being the last locomotives to be built at

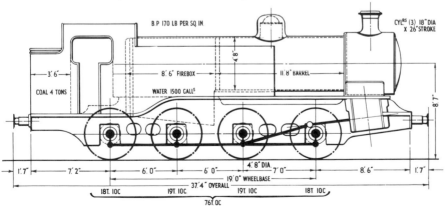

Drawing of proposed 0-8-0T, 1919. *Crown Copyright, National Railway Museum, York*

Cowlairs. Gresley did not attempt to interfere with the order, although the 'N15' was never a class which he envisaged multiplying of his own volition.

Earlier, in 1919, Gresley had considered a 3-cylinder superheated 0-8-0T, considerably more powerful than the 'J50'. It is not clear where this putative design would have been employed, but although two variations were outlined, it did not receive serious attention, and the proposal was not pursued.

However, he later added to two pre-grouping classes introduced for hump shunting duties. It was thought in some quarters that a leading bogie was a useful adjunct to a heavy shunting engine, particularly one used as a pusher, since the bogie tended to throw more weight on to the driving wheels, thus avoiding slipping. The NER evidently followed this view as in 1909 Wilson Worsdell introduced a 3-cylinder 4-8-0T for use in yards in the north-east, LNER Class T1, the original ten being the last locomotives to be constructed at Gateshead Works before NER locomotive building was concentrated at Darlington. Additional heavy shunting power was needed after the grouping, and five more were turned out from Darlington (Nos 1656-60) in 1925 to substantially the same design. Robinson, on the other hand, had adopted the 0-8-4T type (LNER 'S1'), but this was perhaps not so perverse as this class generally worked bunker first up the hump. In 1932, the new Whitemoor Yard, near March, needed hump shunters, so Gresley added to the stock of 'S1s' by building two at Gorton (Nos 2798/9), adding to their capability by providing them with a booster working on to their bogie wheels, which were coupled together. These LNER examples followed the 'J50' feature of sloping tops to their side tanks. Two further 'S1s' were authorised for construction in 1932, but these were subsequently cancelled.

At the other end of the shunting engine scale, a need arose in the North Eastern Area for additional, smaller, shunters, and again Gresley saw no reason to develop a new design from scratch, and in 1925 Doncaster built 10 of the NER 0-6-0T first introduced by Wilson Worsdell in 1898. Classed J72, with 4ft $1\frac{1}{4}$in coupled wheels, and tractive effort no more than 16,760lb, they were the smallest conventional locomotives to be built to Gresley's orders, and were almost exactly to the North Eastern drawings. Proposals for further batches were cancelled or replaced by even smaller locomotives built by the Sentinel Wagon Works at Shrewsbury. These were diminutive engines which owed nothing to Gresley's design influence, but everything to his ability to see that for very light duties suitable locomotives could be bought-in cheaper than they could be designed and built. The Sentinels were 0-4-0Ts, of Classes Y1 and Y3, with power units similar to those of the earliest Sentinel steam railcars. 56 were purchased between 1925 and 1933, including nine for use in Departmental service. A feature of the Sentinels was the vertical boiler, possessing only 64sq ft of heating surface (later examples were somewhat larger), but pressed to 275lb/sq in. The two cylinders were $6\frac{3}{4}$in × 9in, and the driving wheels 2ft 6in in diameter, the 'Y3s' having the advantage of a two-speed gearbox to allow higher speed for running light from shed to yard. Despite their smallness and need for specialised maintenance, the Sentinels achieved a respectable life-span of 20 to 30 years, although in their latter days few were kept hard at work; some spent several years in store, or were loaned to industrial firms for short periods. In retrospect probably the Sentinels were too small for much of the work expected of them, but they saved the LNER money at a time when it was particularly short, and their fuel consumption was low. Two others, Class Y10, were bought in 1930 to work on the Wisbech & Upwell Tramway. These were in effect double engines, but they did not possess the overload capability to deal with the seasonal fruit traffic on this line, and had only a very short life on this duty, being transferred to shunting work and replaced by the Great Eastern tram engines they had been intended to supersede.

An interesting type never to come to fruition was the 2-8-2T, which Gresley seriously considered on two occasions as a replacement for the Ivatt 'R1' 0-8-2T on short haul mineral trains, mainly in the Nottingham district. Each of these proposals reached the stage of inclusion in a formal building programme, but in the event both were cancelled, by a combination of economic depression, the availability of ex-WD 2-8-0s, and possibly the opposition of the Operating Department, preferring the greater range of the '04s' to the drawback of having to turn them at each journey's end. The first proposal was a tank version of the 3-cylinder '02' 2-8-0, 12 of which, described simply as 'P' class, were authorised in the 1930 programme, to replace 14 'R1s'. (An alternative considered at the time would have been smaller, with a 'K2' boiler.) These were cancelled the following year, to be succeeded in the 1932 programme by another 10, this time again with a smaller boiler but based on that fitted to the 'V1' 2-6-2Ts, and referred to as 'P10s'. Two years later these in turn were cancelled, to be replaced in the programme by a batch of eight '02s'.

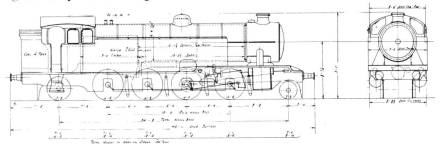

Drawing of proposed 2-8-2T, 1929. Equivalent tank engine version of Class 02.
Crown Copyright, National Railway Museum, York

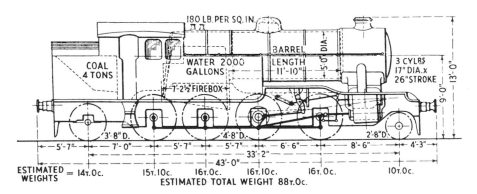

Drawing of proposed 2-8-2T, 1931. Smaller version with 'V1' boiler.

89

Gresley's largest ever design, in fact the biggest and most powerful locomotive built for service on a British railway, was his Class U1 2-8-0+0-8-2 Garratt, No 2395, built to provide banking assistance for mineral trains on the Worsborough incline near Wath. The need for a banking engine stronger than the standard Great Central classes had been considered as long ago as 1910, and when Robinson produced his well-known 2-8-0, he discussed with Beyer Peacock the possibilities of combining a pair of these in a Garratt type. (He had also considered a 0-10-2T, based on his 0-8-4T hump shunter.) No progress however was made by the Great Central — the war intervened, and possibly the GC Board baulked at the expenditure. But the proposal was revived soon after the grouping and Gresley, always willing to try his hand at a big engine, reopened discussions with Beyer Peacock. His initial consideration was in fact for two Garratts, retaining the twin '04' configuration, and he obtained authority to negotiate on a figure of £20,000 for the pair; Beyer Peacock responded by quoting £14,395 each for three. Gresley then realised that if he was to be responsible for Britain's largest locomotive, it would be preferable if it bore his characteristics rather than those of Robinson, so the design was amended to comprise in effect a pair of 3-cylinder '02s', supplied with steam by one massive boiler. In the event, only one was built, for £14,895; it was turned out in time to be a major attraction at the 1925 Stockton & Darlington Centenary celebrations. Although its career was not without problems, it settled down to steady employment at Worsborough until, with electrification of the MS&W, it was transferred in 1949 to Bromsgrove for work on the Lickey incline. Here it was cordially disliked by its crews, and after a further period during which it was fired by oil, it was withdrawn at the end of 1955. At Worsborough, the alternative to the Garratt was a pair of '04s', which in 1925 were being bought from the disposal agency for £1,500 each, excluding reconditioning, and although No 2395 saved the cost of a crew and presumably burned less coal than two 2-8-0s, it is difficult to visualise these savings offsetting the Garratt's higher capital cost, plus the maintenance costs of that unique boiler — which incidentally was never renewed, lasting thirty years, as long as the locomotive itself.

On his assumption of office in April 1941, Edward Thompson found that 10 'J50s' had been included in the building programme for 1940, but that whilst material was being assembled, and parts fabricated, construction had not commenced. At the same time, a number of Great Central 'Q4' 0-8-0s were scheduled for withdrawal, and he considered that he could produce a more powerful shunting tank than the 'J50s' and at the same time save steel by converting a number of these 'Q4s' to 0-8-0Ts. Material already prepared for the 'J50s' could be used in the conversion (which explains some of the similarities in appearance of the two classes) whilst the tenders could be re-used to provide new ones for locomotives under construction. Although the 'Q4s' were between 30 and 40 years old at the time of conversion, the original frames, and probably the original cylinders, wheel centres and rods were retained, a striking tribute to the ruggedness of locomotives built by Robinson. A saving of £2,050 per engine over the 'J50s' was postulated, apart from the bonus of the tenders, but despite this new lease of life, the 'Q1s', as the conversions were classed, could not have been expected to last as long as new engines. Nevertheless, as a resource-saving measure in wartime, the conversion had much to commend it, although only 13 of the 25 authorised were actually rebuilt, and the class does not appear to have been received with a great deal of favour, except for those engaged in short distance transfer work in the Frodingham locality.

Both the 'Q1' and the 'J50' featured in Thompson's published postwar plan, the 'J50' being the only Gresley design to continue to be built. Thompson's light shunting tank was unspecified, but earlier considerations had once more mentioned the 'J72', which in the event was revived by Peppercorn and Harrison, no fewer than 28 being built at Darlington in 1949-51, despite the prospect of an influx of diesel-electric shunters.

The final tank engine class to be taken into LNER service was again of an outside derivation. In 1946, 75 ex-War Department 0-6-0STs were acquired, of a design owing nothing to Doncaster or Darlington, but originating with the Hunslet Locomotive Company of Leeds, and again obviating the need for additional 'J50s'. The boiler was rather smaller than that of the 'J50', having 960sq ft of heating surface. With 170lb/sq in boiler pressure, 18in×26in cylinders and coupled wheels no larger than 4ft 3in diameter, tractive effort was 23,870lb. The full length saddle tank had a capacity of 1,200 gallons. Classified J94, and numbered 8006-80 in the later LNER series, they mainly worked in the North Eastern Area, and around Immingham, giving way to the ubiquitous BR diesel-electric shunters in the 1960s.

The history of the construction of shunting tanks for the LNER is an interesting commentary on locomotive practice, in which coherent development took second place to enforced financial pragmatism. Gresley inherited the traditional Stirling/Ivatt shunter, improved it, and continued to build it until 1939. It was proposed for postwar construction by Thompson, and no doubt could have met almost all of the shunting duties on the railway. But the availability of outside designs at lower cost, completely non-standard with any LNER components, together with Thompson's desire to demonstrate his ability to give new life to old engines, and finally the latter-day reversion to another 19th century basic design, all combined to make a nonsense of any considerations of a single class of shunting tank. It is a final irony that the 'J94' reverted to the saddle tank, a feature rejected by Gresley.

Above: BR No 60162 *Saint Johnstoun* at Haymarket, September 1953. The last of the line, the final Peppercorn Pacific. *J. Robertson*

Right: Southern Railway No 21C1 *Channel Packet*. Bulleid's original 'Merchant Navy' Pacific. The Gresley influence is not obvious. *IAL*

Below: No 71000 *Duke of Gloucester*. Note the drive to the Caprotti valves, 3-bar slide bars and crosshead. *IAL*

Above: No 2545 *Diamond Jubilee* at Kings Cross shed 1926. *F. R. Hebron/Rail Archive Stephenson*

Below: No 4489 *Dominion of Canada* at Grantham, June 1938. Steam operated bell presented by Canadian Pacific Railway. *T. G. Hepburn/Rail Archive Stephenson*

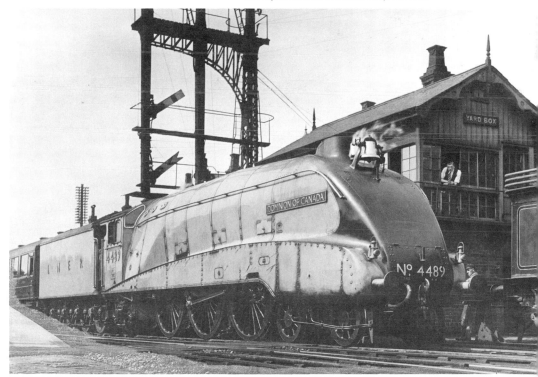

Top: No 3284 on up 'West Riding Pullman' at New Barnet, September 1934. Ivatt Atlantic modified by Gresley with piston valves and superheater. *Wethersett Collection/IAL*

Left: No 6385 *Luckie Mucklebackit*. Robinson 'Director' class built by Kitson & Co in 1924 for service in Scotland. *Real Photos*

Below left: No 269 *The Cleveland*. 'Hunt' class with poppet valves. Built at Darlington, 1932. *IAL*

Top right: No 307 *Kincardineshire*, 'Shire' class with piston valves. On train of green and cream tourist stock. *IAL*

Centre right: No 8572. One of the 1928 Beyer Peacock batch with Lentz poppet valves. *Crown Copyright, National Railway Museum, York*

Right: No 8579 rebuilt as 'B12/3' on down slow Cambridge train at Shepreth, July 1933. *Wethersett Collection/IAL*

Above: No 2867 *Bradford*. A 'Footballer' on the 5pm from Marylebone at Chorley Wood, June 1939. *Wethersett Collection*

Left: No 8900 *Claud Hamilton* rebuilt by Gresley with round topped firebox as Class D16/3. *Real Photos*

Below: BR No 61671 *Royal Sovereign* rebuilt by Thompson as Class B2, on up slow train of quad-arts, July 1953. *Real Photos*

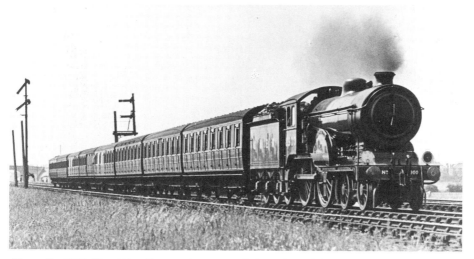

Above No 8900 *Claud Hamilton* on down Southend train at Chadwell Heath, May 1935. *Wethersett Collection/IAL*

Below: One of the 'Royal Clauds' No 8783 before being rebuilt by Gresley. On up Cambridge train at New Southgate, May 1933. *Wethersett Collection/IAL*

Above: No 365 *The Morpeth* rebuilt by Thompson with inside cylinders, 1942. *Crown Copyright National Railway Museum, York*

Left: No 1653N (LNER interim numbering) Class K2. 2-bar slide bars and heavyweight crosshead, and piston tail rods. *L&GRP, courtesy David & Charles*

Below: No 2427, Class K3, climbing to Potters Bar with down fitted goods train, June 1936. *Wethersett Collection/IAL*

Above: No 3442 *The Great Marquess*, Class K4, as restored. Seen at Wetherby, September 1963. Bell from Pennsylvania 'K4s' class. Now owned by Lord Garnock. *G. W. Morrison*

Below: No 846 at York, July 1946. Gresley rebuild of Raven 4-6-0 as 'B16/2'. *Wethersett Collection/IAL*

Top: No 3401 *Bantam Cock* on down
express at Trumpington, August 1941.
Wethersett Collection/IAL

Above: No 3442 *The Great Marquess*
piloting 'K1' No 62005 on a rail tour special
at Bridlington, March 1965. *D. Hardy*

Below: Thompson 'B1' No 1059, new from
North British Loco Co, at Eastfield, July
1946. *Wethersett Collection/IAL*

Above: 'B1' No 1099 on down outer suburban train at New Southgate, August 1948. *Wethersett Collection/IAL*

Left: No 206, Class K5. Thompson 2-cylinder conversion. *Crown Copyright, National Railway Museum, York*

Below: 'K3' No 1164 in Nottingham Victoria station with up train of green and cream excursion stock. *T. G. Hepburn/Rail Archive Stephenson*

Right: No 3464 Gresley 2-cylinder 2-8-0. Note drive onto third pair of coupled wheels. *Real Photos*

Below: GNR No 477, original production version of 3-cylinder 2-8-0, Class 02. *Real Photos*

Bottom: No 2959 of the 1932 batch of '02s', the first to be built with side window cabs. *Real Photos*

Above: Class O2 No 2431 on up goods train at Littlebury, July 1934. Note 50ton brick wagon. *Wethersett Collection/IAL*

Left: No 6617, classic Robinson 2-8-0 of LNER Class O4. This example was built by NBL in 1919 to Government order for some £9,000, hired to the LNWR in 1919/21 and left in a dump at Queensferry until bought by the LNER in 1927 for £340. After overhaul it entered LNER service in 1928. *IAL*

Below: No 6314, Robinson 'O4' in original condition. *Real Photos*

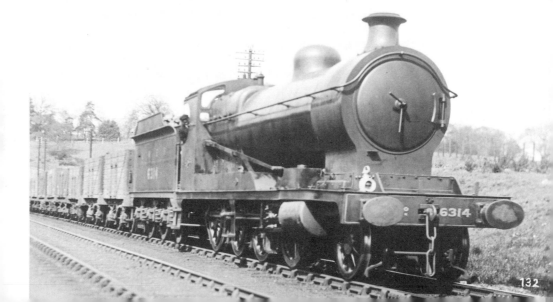

Chapter 9
Electric and Diesel Traction

In his Presidential Address to the Institution of Locomotive Engineers in 1927, Nigel Gresley reminded his professional colleagues that 'We are the Institution of Locomotive Engineers, not the Institution of Steam Locomotive Engineers. All kinds of locomotives, steam, oil and electric are our concern'. He had great expectations of cheap electrical energy, and if these could be realised, the fields for electrification would be extended. Nevertheless he thought that improvements would be made in internal combustion and steam locomotives, so that they would be able to maintain their position as economic forms of transport.

These statesmanlike views disclosed an aspect of Gresley which is not generally appreciated: most observers believe that, being the dedicated steam locomotive engineer he so obviously was, his mind was closed to other forms of traction. True, in the economics of the period, when coal (in today's terms) was cheap, and the LNER earned substantial revenue from moving it about the system, and whilst finance for investment in electrification was virtually non-existent, coal fired steam locomotives necessarily provided the main source of motive power. It is also true that Gresley professed little knowledge of the technology of electrification, referring to electric locomotives as 'wireless boxes on wheels', but in H. W. H. Richards he had an electrical engineer who was amongst the leading experts of the day on railway electrification, and who would have furnished the LNER with many miles of electrified system had the opportunity been provided. Indeed, in 1928, when cutbacks were the order of the day, Richards' staff was strengthened to deal with the preparation of a number of electric traction schemes, commencing with the GN suburban lines. Another sidelight on Gresley's interest in electric traction may be discerned in a contribution he made in 1923 at a meeting of the Institution of Electrical Engineers. The subject was the electrification of the French Midi Railway, and he observed that it was important from a railway company's point of view that it should possess a co-operative interest in the electricity supply system, to avoid placing itself in the hands of the power company.

The Great Eastern and the Great Northern had considered suburban electrification as far back as the early 1900s, but in neither instance did it appear that the finance could be justified. Indeed, the case against electrification was bolstered by somewhat spurious claims by certain locomotive engineers of the day, particularly when Fred V. Russell designed the well-known Decapod for

James Holden, said to have possessed the acceleration of electric traction, but which was an impossibility to operate.

The LNER Board had revived the question of electrification of the Great Northern suburban services in the first year of grouping, considering proposals for the main line as far as Hitchin, and for the branch lines. Because of the need for compatibility with the Metropolitan system, it was thought that the inner suburban lines would be operated at 650V dc, the quad-art sets having been designed to be readily convertible to multiple-unit operation. From Potters Bar to Hitchin the system would be 1,500V dc, no doubt with further electrification in mind. Express passenger and fish trains would continue to be steam operated, but outer suburban, coal and goods trains would be hauled by electric traction, a changeover point being established at Hitchin. Provision was made for 20 80ton electric locomotives, designed for dual 650/1,500V supply. To complete a trio of CME's involved in the discussions, not only were Raven (as Technical Adviser) and Gresley present, but also C. E. Fairburn, then representing the manufacturers English Electric, and later to join the LMS. Financial stringency caused shelving of the proposals in 1925, but they were revived in 1930, although it was then made clear that any progress would depend upon adequate assistance being forthcoming from the Government. At a cost of nearly £4½ million for the Great Northern scheme, electrification was then reckoned to save 60 steam engines, but even assuming 100% increase in traffic, a return of only 6% was envisaged. However the Government New Works programme later in the decade, loaning money to the railways at low interest, enabled a start to be made on the relief of the GE and GN suburban systems, under which certain services would be transferred to the London Transport Underground network, and the GE main line electrified as far as Shenfield. But the bulk of the outer suburban services from Kings Cross and Liverpool Street had to wait until well into the British Railways era, overhead electrification reaching Clacton in 1962 and Royston in 1980, respectively completing the Great Eastern and Great Northern conversions, at least for the time being. Originally reaching Shenfield at 1,500V dc, later construction was to the postwar standard of 25kV 50Hz ac, to which the Shenfield line was eventually changed.

Electrification had achieved reality much earlier in the north-east, the lines to Tynemouth having been converted to 600V third rail as far back as 1904. The Shildon to Newport mineral line followed in 1915, this time at 1,500V overhead, and 10 Bo-Bo locomotives were built to run the trains; two smaller Bo-Bos were also introduced to operate the short electrified branch to Newcastle Quayside. However the North Eastern Board were far-seeing in electrification, and a report in 1919 recommended conversion of the line from York to Newcastle, at 1,500V dc, with a well argued case for third rail on the main lines and overhead in the yards. Twenty passenger and 87 freight locomotives were postulated, one of which was actually built. Surely the most expensive white elephant in British railway history, a 2-C-2 was constructed at a cost originally estimated at £20,000 (later put by Stamer at £27,767), but apart from early acceptance trials on the Shildon-Newport line, and a brief appearance in the Centenary parade in 1925, towed by 'J71' No 1163, it languished at Darlington until it was quietly sold for scrapping by BR in 1950. Electrification of the NER main line would probably have become a reality had the grouping not taken place, but the topic was never considered by the LNER Board, despite the strong North Eastern influence it retained. The Shildon-Newport line reverted to steam in 1935, by which time the traffic had fallen to 15% of that in 1913, when the electrification was planned.

Three Committees were set up by the Government in the 1920s to consider railway electrification, the most important being the Weir Committee, established in 1929, with Sir Ralph Wedgwood as the only member who was a railwayman. The Committee concluded that the only way in which full benefit would accrue would be by electrification of the entire railway system. In reaching this conclusion, two possible electrification schemes at 1,500V dc were surveyed and costed: the LMS lines from Crewe to Liverpool and Carlisle, and the LNER Kings Cross to Leeds route, plus the branches to Nottingham, Grimsby and March. The cost of the LNER project was put at £8.6 million, a return of 7.22% on the investment being predicted, earned entirely by cost savings, no allowance being included for additional business generated by the electrification. In a period when interest rates generally were in low single figures, hindsight might consider there would have been some future for the scheme, but in the depths of the 1931 depression no political enthusiasm could be engendered for such proposals.

Nevertheless some progress was made in 1931, as in that year electrification of the Manchester, South Junction and Altrincham suburban line was completed, in which the LNER were partners with the LMS. However, the only electrified line for which Gresley was fully responsible for the rolling stock was the North Tyneside system, new multiple-unit stock being provided in 1937. The original coaches were renovated and transferred to the newly electrified South Tyneside line to South Shields.

However a major step forward was taken in the mid-1930s, when as a further part of the Government New Works programme, at a cost of £1.6 million in contemporary values, and calculated to return 10% on the investment, a major programme was initiated for the electrification of the Manchester, Sheffield and Wath line over the Pennines, including the formidable 1 in 40 of the Worsborough incline. It was originally estimated that this would call for 25 passenger, 64 freight and 32 shunting and banking engines (including conversion of the Shildon Bo-Bos), replacing 196 steam locomotives, and Gresley instructed Richards to develop a suitable design of freight engine, conscious that this would be a pioneer of its kind in Britain. The project was taken in hand by A. G. Hopking and A. H. Emerson, of the Electrical Engineer's staff, in conjunction with leading British manufacturers, and a consensus emerged that a Bo-Bo locomotive could be developed capable of handling a trailing load of 1,090 tons, with banking assistance up the Worsborough incline. However, when tests took place later, it was discovered that difficulty would be encountered not in hauling loose-coupled unbraked trains of this weight, but in stopping them in an emergency; because of this, rheostatic braking was added to the regenerative braking system already provided, but nevertheless the maximum trailing load had to be reduced to 700 tons. This removed the need for special banking engines, and apart from one which was modernised after the war and later used on carriage shunting in connection with the Shenfield electrification, the Shildon Bo-Bos were sold for scrap.

Whilst the proposal for an electric freight locomotive for the MS&W was under investigation, Gresley's attention was drawn to a system which had been developed for diesel or electric bogie locomotives in which the drawbar pull was taken not through the locomotive body, but through the bogie frames, involving a complex system of coupling between the bogies. This had been incorporated in a class of locomotives exported to South Africa, and Gresley decided to see these in action for himself. He returned convinced that the idea was sound, and eventually tenders were invited for construction of the new engines, designed by the LNER electrical engineering staff, but incorporating proprietary equipment. Metropolitan Vickers secured the contract and the prototype, No 6701, Class EM1, was completed in February 1941 and was unveiled in York Old Station Yard at the same press conference as the 'V4' *Bantam Cock*. In a unique bi-national experience, No 6701 ran on the Netherlands railway system between 1947 and 1952, being officially dubbed *Tommy* in commemoration; as a result of this extensive testing many modifications were introduced in the 57 production 'EM1s' which followed, up to 1953. Nevertheless these were recognisably to the original Gresley specification and many remained in service until closure of the Woodhead tunnel route in 1981. So, a Gresley designed locomotive class lasted long enough to be painted rail blue, and to bear the BR motif.

In later years it was found that the bogie coupling system had certain drawbacks which led to rough riding, and on a number of occasions bent centre pins were reported. When the passenger variety was finally introduced in 1953, Class EM2, reversion was made to conventional bogie design, similar in many aspects to that of the prototype English Electric diesel-electrics built in 1947 for the LMS, and leading to a Co-Co wheel arrangement. In the event, only seven were built, and on their withdrawal in 1968/9, following their redundancy on the MS&W as a result of the cessation of passenger services, the 'EM2s' were sold to the Netherlands Railways.

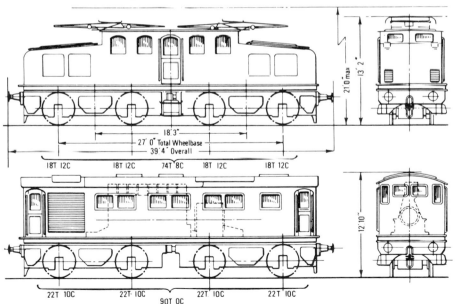

Proposed Bo-Bo diesel-electric conversion of Shildon electric locomotive.

In early LNER days the contemporary technology of electrification was proven; the obstacle to its wider application was financial. However the rapidly developing oil engine industry had not yet succeeded in adapting its products to conditions on the railways, and indeed in a country with the coal resources of Great Britain, the case for motive power based on imported oil would have been difficult to sustain, even if the technology had been proved. Nevertheless, as a further example of Nigel Gresley's wider outlook, he told the LNER Locomotive Committee in 1928 that he had been closely following the development of the diesel engine, and its application to locomotive purposes. This led to a most interesting proposal, in which one of the then redundant Shildon-Newport Bo-Bo electrics was to be converted to diesel-electric operation as a prototype of a fleet of such locomotives, intended to haul the New England-Ferme Park coal trains. A cost/benefit calculation based on somewhat questionable assumptions showed a saving of 24% on train-mile costs, coal in those days being reckoned at £1 a ton, and oil £4.50 a ton. The prime mover was to have been a 1,000hp 900rpm Beardmore diesel engine, driving an English Electric generator which in turn supplied 1,500V dc to the four 275hp motors of the Bo-Bo. This seems to have been an engineering nonsense, and one wonders how those concerned convinced themselves of the merits of the proposal in the first place, but it foundered anyway the following year when the realisation sunk in that a much larger diesel engine would be needed, but that the frame would not support the additional weight.

At the time, the main effort in diesel engine design was in applications for marine purposes, intended for continuous operation at low speeds. To fit a power unit of 2,000hp or more into the restricted space permitted by the British loading gauge called for a higher speed design than was currently available. Consequently early excursions into the employment of diesel engines contemplated relatively low powered units.

In 1931, the Belfast firm of Harland & Wolff submitted proposals for two small diesel-electric locomotives. The larger of these was a Bo-Bo type, rated at 450hp, and referred to as a 'tractor'; the smaller was described as a 'shunting tractor', weighing 40 tons and carried on six wheels. No great interest appears to have been shown by the LNER in either, although the manufacturers went to the trouble of submitting drawings painted green and lettered LNER.

Gresley's first venture into actual diesel-electric hardware came in 1933, when an experimental 880hp Armstrong-Whitworth 1-C-1 was tested in the North Eastern Area, but this was unsuccessful on account of high axle loading and excessive rigidity. A 6-coupled shunter was tried at the same time, but compared with the LMS, the LNER was late in the introduction of diesel-electric shunting locomotives. Four 350hp units were ordered in 1941, but were not put into traffic until 1944/5; these were constructed at Doncaster, the equipment being supplied by English Electric. As a wartime measure, changeover switching was installed on each locomotive to allow the generator to provide an emergency supply of electricity to an external load, such as a workshop.

In the meantime, earlier in the decade, in 1932, another unconventional idea was considered, in which drawings were made of an Ivatt 'R1' 0-8-2T converted to diesel/compressed air operation. A 400hp diesel engine was to drive an air compressor, and steam was to be produced from a small boiler heated by the diesel exhaust, compressed air and steam being fed into the cylinders. There may have been some distant relationship with the Kitson-Still 2-6-2T private venture of 1928 in which, in a double acting engine, steam acted on one side of the cylinders to start the locomotive, and, when running, power was provided by diesel compression-ignition acting on the other side of the cylinders. This experimental machine ran trials on the LNER during the years following its introduction, but no more was heard of the proposed 'R1' conversion.

By 1939, there had been a substantial advance in the technology of the diesel engine, and in consideration of this, and the possibility of lesser availability of good quality locomotive coal, Gresley initiated a study intended to produce a design specification for a medium power mixed traffic diesel-electric locomotive. No details were published, however, and the war intervened to prevent the project from being taken very far.

In a brave show of intent in the last year of the LNER's independent existence, a report was considered of the merits of gas-turbine operation, whilst the Board also discussed in some depth the possibilities of introducing a fleet of diesel-electric locomotives. 25 1,600hp units, to be used in tandem, were envisaged as replacing 32 Pacifics on Anglo-Scottish services, and this proposal went as far as the tendering stage, one of the last acts of Sir Ronald Matthews, as Chairman, being to open the tenders submitted by six manufacturers. But there the matter was left in abeyance, and diesel-electric traction on the Eastern and North Eastern Regions had to await the BR modernisation plan. The three classes of locomotive then mostly in evidence were the 2,000hp English Electric Class 40s, the 2,750hp Brush-Sulzer Class 47s, and the 3,300hp English Electric Class 55s, the 'Deltics', the latter being amongst the most powerful passenger locomotives ever to run on a British railway. The 'Deltics' enabled the East Coast main line to lead the country in high speed rail travel for 15 years; one feels that Sir Nigel would have approved.

Chapter 10

Locomotive Design: Steam Generation

Locomotive design under Nigel Gresley was approached in two stages. First he would define the traffic objectives of the locomotive under consideration, and the conditions under which it would operate; these would be gone into with Bulleid, and later Edge, and with Spencer, his technical assistant. Alternative ways of meeting these requirements would be considered in general terms, often with Gresley sketching an outline on his drawing pad. When provisional decisions had been taken on the form of the new design, the main dimensions would be firmed up and approximate calculations made of weights and adhesion factor, and the approval of the Civil Engineer obtained. Then, the agreed outline would be sent to the drawing office — generally Doncaster, but in earlier LNER years Darlington was used for certain projects such as the 'J39' and 'D49'. The drawing office would work up the design in detail, eg drawing the outlines of the frames, after the necessary stress calculations had been made, deciding how best to fit the tubes and flues into the boiler, for which the throat plate and back plate positions had been fixed by the CME, and generally completing the design so that it could be translated into hardware in the locomotive works. The amount of complex detail work involved in completing the drawings of a new class before materials could be ordered and construction put in hand was such that instructions were rarely issued to the drawing office unless there was every expectation of the project going ahead. Like all locomotive engineers, Gresley considered a great many proposals which in the event were unfulfilled, although outline drawings give an indication of the existence of some of these 'might have beens'. Many such drawings were variations of the same basic design, incorporating modifications and improvements as the design progressed. Bulleid has said that Gresley was quicker than any other man he knew in his ability to read a drawing, and whilst a design was going through the drawing office, the CME would intervene personally from time to time to check or change some aspect which took his eye. In this he departed from the practice of many of his contemporaries on other railways who after giving general instructions left virtually the entire design to the Chief Draughtsman. Men such as W. M. Smith on the North Eastern, S. Rowlands on the Great Central, and Fred V. Russell, Great Eastern, gave such support to their respective chiefs, who took final responsibility for the design, and the credit (and occasionally the opprobium) which followed. The story is vouched for that J. G. Robinson, having issued orders for his next 4-6-0 to have four cylinders, took

R. A. Thom, then his assistant, to task for not having fulfilled his wishes. When he first heard the engine in motion, evidently Robinson thought it should have eight beats per wheel revolution, and explanatory diagrams had to be drawn in chalk on the floor of Gorton works.

Throughout his working life in charge of locomotive design, Gresley followed the principle expounded by Ivatt that what an engine needed most was plenty of steam. In considering the source of heat needed to generate this steam, Gresley was a staunch advocate of the round topped firebox, as opposed to the square topped Belpaire type favoured by Churchward, Stanier and Riddles. In the absence of any definitive comparative trials, a choice can only be made from subjective judgment, and Gresley believed that the lower cost of construction and maintenance of the round topped version outweighed any unproven advantage in steam raising. Although the pre-grouping Doncaster and Darlington schools agreed on the round topped type, the Great Eastern and Great Central had adopted the Belpaire style. Also, exceptionally, the two Smith compounds built in 1906 for the North Eastern, and the successive batches of North British Atlantics, were fitted with Belpaire fireboxes. When under Gresley a major rebuilding took place, as with the Great Eastern 'B12s' and 'Clauds', as well as their 'J18/19/20' 0-6-0s and on the Great Central, Robinson's 'O4s', a round topped firebox was substituted for the original Belpaire. Further, when in 1927/8 the last batch of 'N7s' to GE design were being constructed at Doncaster, a round topped firebox was provided, this pattern being eventually fitted as a replacement to all but two of the class. But when other pre-grouping locomotive designs were perpetuated in new building, even as late as the 1928 'B12s' and the 1932 'S1s', no round topped firebox was substituted for the original, nor was there any serious attempt to replace Belpaire boxes on other older locomotives as the originals wore out. One perhaps obvious candidate for conversion was the GCR 'Director' class of 4-4-0, on which the boiler fitted to the 'J39s' and 'D49s' would have been a fair substitute for the original. Indeed, in his early standardisation considerations, Thompson — who did not disagree with Gresley over firebox and boiler design — had included this class along with the 'D49s', rebuilt to two cylinders, as the prototype for his 6ft 8in class of 4-4-0. Strangely, at a meeting of the Institution of Locomotive Engineers in November 1924, Spencer is on record as expressing surprise that the Belpaire firebox was not used in Britain to a greater extent, as although construction cost was slightly greater than that of the round type, there were many other advantages. Presumably in this aspect of design, he did not press his apparent disagreement with Gresley. In fact Belpaire fireboxes were not to be built at Doncaster until Stanier 2-8-0s were turned out to Government order during World War 2.

Following the successful introduction of the wide grate firebox, based on the American Wootten type, on the large Ivatt Atlantics, Gresley applied this to his Pacifics and Mikados, and to the 'V2s', all big engines with a high required rate of firing. Whether the expense was worthwhile on his smaller 2-6-2, the 'V4', is conjectural, whilst the proposal for a 2-6-4T version of the 'V4', also with a wide firebox, did not get beyond the drawing board.

Despite his acceptance of Ivatt's dictum on the need for plenty of steam, Gresley's first GNR 2-6-0 was underboilered, a deficiency to be remedied two years later, and not to be repeated. Indeed, his 1920 2-6-0 design featured a 6ft diameter boiler, the largest seen in Britain up to then. For most of his time he adhered to a parallel boiler design for all but his largest locomotives, to which he applied the tapered boiler style featured in Swindon practice and in the Pennsylvania 'K4s', initially on his Pacific of 1922, which had a boiler 6ft 5in in diameter at the firebox end, reducing to 5ft 9in halfway along the barrel. This use of the tapered boiler in his largest engines contrasts with Swindon (and later BR) practice in which many smaller classes were also fitted with a taper boiler. However a possible change in Gresley's attitude was indicated by the application of a taper boiler to his last design, the 'V4', but this was probably dictated by the choice, for this class, of a wide firebox.

A feature of a wide firebox, compared with one with a narrow grate, is that to achieve a comparable ratio of volume to grate area, the firebox must be extended into the boiler barrel in the form of a combustion chamber. This provides valuable additional heating surface, but its presence gives rise to the need for the boiler barrel to have a tapered ring adjacent to the firebox to allow adequate space for steam and water above the firebox, unless the boiler is to be oversized at the front end. Apart from this, a taper has the advantage of reducing the specific weight of the boiler at the front end, which being cooler and contributing less to steam generation, may be less in diameter than the firebox end, where most steam is generated.

Gresley incorporated these principles in his original Pacific boiler, adapting to British conditions a form of construction which had become current American practice, and which was exemplified in the Pennsylvania 'K4s'. The 6ft 5in diameter boiler made the most of the space available within the limitations imposed by the position of the coupled wheels and the load gauge, providing ample volume for water and steam around the combustion chamber. At the front end, space had to be provided beneath the boiler for the inside cylinder and motion, the cylinder being included at 1 in 8 to allow the drive to be on to the middle coupled axle. Consequently the Gresley boiler tapered towards the front end on a horizontal axis, differing from the Churchward and 'K4s' designs in which there was a downward slope of the axis, with the taper appearing all at the top of the boiler, and so permitting a longer chimney and somewhat improved visibility from the cab.

Incorporation of the combustion chamber enabled Gresley to keep the tube length of the Pacific's boiler down to 19ft, compared with the overlong 20ft of the Raven Pacific, whilst when the 'A4' was developed the tube length was reduced to 17ft 11$\frac{3}{4}$in, this being compensated for by an equivalent enlargement of the combustion chamber. The resulting heating surface was slightly reduced on the original, but the 'A4s' were reputed to have been even better steamers than the 'A3s'. All in all, Gresley's 1922 Pacific boiler was the first example of a compact form of a large boiler with a wide firebox, and as such served as a prototype for subsequent development not only on the LNER but also on the LMS and Southern Railways. It represented one of his major contributions to locomotive development.

Gresley's attitude to the question of boiler pressure was for many years on the conservative side, and he was reluctant to move very much from the 170lb/sq in of Ivatt's day, on the basis that this was all that was necessary, and increased pressure only meant higher construction and maintenance costs; even his first

Pacifics only had 180lb/sq in pressure. A fair enough argument, until the 1925 exchange trials with the 225lb/sq in in 'Castles' seemed to indicate that there was perhaps some advantage to be gained from a higher pressure. Acceptance of the point led, after trials in which two Pacifics were fitted with 220lb boilers, to the 'A3' design of 1928, and later to the 250lb/sq in of the 'A4s' (and the 275lb/sq in of the unfulfilled further development). Other designs to exceed 180lb/sq in were the 200lb/sq in 'B17s', the NB Loco Co design which required this higher pressure to achieve the specified tractive effort, and the 'P2s' and 'V2s', which followed the 'A3' figure of 220lb. Of Gresley's last small engine classes, the 'V3' 2-6-2T and the 'K4' 2-6-0 had 200lb/sq in boilers, whilst *Bantam Cock* went to 250lb. The water-tube boiler of No 10000 was of course an exception at 450lb/sq in.

The technique of superheating had become established by the time of Ivatt's retirement, the Schmidt form of superheater being in general vogue. Gresley was concerned to fit what he believed to be the most effective pattern, and soon after taking charge at Doncaster he fitted five of the last 10 large Atlantics with 24 element Schmidt superheaters in place of the original 18 element type. This was followed in 1914 by the introduction of the Robinson superheater, again with 24 elements, to another Atlantic. The Robinson pattern had the advantage of being more easily maintained in a steamtight condition, and from 1918 onwards most of the Atlantics received 32 element Robinson superheaters. Gresley also developed a type of superheater to his own design, for which he obtained a patent; this had a twin-tube arrangement, and was fitted to various classes of GNR locomotives. However problems persisted with steamtightness, and although the Gresley pattern was applied in particular to the N2 0-6-2Ts, most of his engines were fitted with the straightforward Robinson type, only differing in the number of elements eg 32 on the 'C1s' and the original 'A1s', 43 on the 'A3s' and 'A4s', and in the length of the elements.

At the other extreme from the large passenger engines, in the early days of his administration on the Great Northern, Gresley was intent on establishing whether superheating would also benefit the shunting tank, and fitted one of his 0-6-0Ts with a Robinson superheater, for evaluation against other members of the class working on saturated steam. A saving of $3\frac{1}{2}$% on coal consumption was claimed, but this was not considered sufficient justification for the class as a whole to receive superheaters. Due to the intermittent nature of their work, it was concluded that the smaller shunting tank engines could not take full advantage of the higher temperatures generated by the superheater. In another experiment, this time with his largest locomotives of the time, a variation known as the 'E' type was obtained from the Superheater Company of New York, and this formed part of an experimental partial retubing of the type of boiler fitted to the 'A1s' and 'P1s'. 124 flues were provided, of $3\frac{1}{2}$in diameter, compared with the standard 32 of $5\frac{1}{4}$in, and 62 elements were threaded into the flues, this assembly being tried on 'A1' No 2562 and 'P1' No 2394 from new. No significant temperature increase was recorded however. Finally, No 10000, as always, was a special case; initially, the superheat temperature of the high pressure steam was found to be too high, and steps had to be taken to reduce it, whilst the low pressure superheat was too low, and was increased.

Chapter 11

Locomotive Design: Steam Utilisation

In the early days of the 20th century it was becoming clear that the British loading gauge precluded large outside cylinders of the size likely to be reached in American practice, yet more cylinder power was needed to cope with increasing train loads. The solution lay in multi-cylindered designs, pioneered in batch production in 1907 by G. J. Churchward in his 'Star' class, which were provided with four cylinders but only two sets of valve gear. Bowen Cooke of the LNWR followed suit in his 'Claughtons', whilst Gresley's thoughts also turned in this direction with his experimental conversion of Atlantic No 279 and his 1915 outline of a Pacific. However, whilst a 4-cylinder locomotive can be made to operate comfortably with only two sets of valve gear, the same cannot easily be said of one with three cylinders. Nevertheless Gresley was attracted by the advantages, as he saw them, of three cylinder propulsion, providing more even torque than two cylinders, and yet saving the weight necessitated by the introduction of a fourth cylinder. A disadvantage lay in the apparent need for a third set of valve gear, and he met this to his satisfaction by designing and patenting in 1915 a method of operating the valves of the inside cylinder by means of a complex system of levers deriving their motion from the outside valve gear.

Gresley's patented system was applied to his first 3-cylinder 2-8-0, No 461, in 1918, in which the three cylinders were all sharply inclined, and both the complexity of the derived gear and the inclination of the cylinders attracted adverse comment. This reached the columns of the 'The Engineer', to which one of Gresley's contemporaries, regrettably anonymously, wrote a series of highly critical letters. However — and Gresley must have been aware of it — H. Holcroft had already patented a similar system whilst working for Churchward at Swindon, but had understandably failed to convince his chief of the merits of this, or that there was anything better for the 'Stars' than straightforward 4-cylinder propulsion. Later, in 1918, Holcroft read a Paper before the Institution of Locomotive Engineers on the subject, and Gresley invited him to discuss the topic with him. Indeed, Holcroft, who by then had moved to the South Eastern & Chatham, was invited to join the Gresley team, but R. E. L. Maunsell, then in charge of locomotive matters on the SE&CR, refused him permission. Presumably this means that Gresley was unable to make a sufficiently attractive offer.

Anyway, the result was that when further Great Northern 3-cylinder locomotives were built, 2-8-0s, 2-6-0s, and finally Pacifics, the derived gear was modified according to Holcroft's suggestions, and when correctly adjusted it worked well. But in service, wear in joints and bearings became cumulative at the inside piston valves, so giving rise to the characteristic syncopated beat of a Gresley engine due for overhaul. With regular attention by skilled fitters, the gear met all requirements, but as wear developed the middle cylinder performed erratically, producing less horsepower than the outside cylinders at low speeds, and more as the speed increased. A further design difficulty lay in the necessity in the larger engines to accommodate the mechanism in front of the cylinders where it was subject to the intrusion of smokebox ash. However in the 'D49s' and 'B17s' the gear could be fitted behind the cylinders, so this aspect of the problem was much less troublesome in these classes. In after years an LNER Southern Area Locomotive Running Superintendent was heard to complain that Darlington never really mastered the art of setting Gresley valves, whilst E. S. Cox has pointed out that leverage in the 2 : 1 arrangement was such that wear at the pins attached to the outside valve spindles could be magnified to become 11 times as much lost motion at the inside valve.

At one time the Americans showed an interest in the Gresley derived gear, and it was fitted to a small number of locomotives built by the American Locomotive Company, (ALCO). However as part of the general US dislike of inside cylinders, the Gresley gear was discontinued on the general grounds of inaccessibility. The locomotives concerned were designed for freight haulage, and ALCO recommended a maximum speed of 35mph.

With the formation of the LNER, and following Sir Vincent Raven's report, responsibility for locomotive maintenance at sheds, between major overhauls, was removed from the CME. Had this continued to lie within his department, stronger messages might have reached Gresley about the shortcomings in service of his derived valve gear; undoubtedly he was aware of the problems, but would have said that there was nothing wrong which couldn't have been overcome by good maintenance. It was to improve such communication, as well as to try to enforce a more uniform standard of maintenance, that the responsibility of the Locomotive Running Superintendents was divided, and whilst they continued to report to the Operating Superintendents for matters concerned with operating the locomotive fleet, oversight of locomotives in the sheds was transferred to the Mechanical Engineer for the Area concerned. It was of course the sheer inability of the shed staff to provide the required quality of maintenance during the war years that gave Thompson the validity of his case for providing his rebuilds of the 'P2s' and No 4470 with three separate sets of Walschaerts valve gear.

Having satisfied himself that the 3-cylinder system was intrinsically satisfactory, in addition to applying it to the largest locomotives, for which it was a necessity, Gresley also adopted it for smaller engines for which two cylinders would have sufficed. Limited comparative tests indicated a slightly lower coal and water consumption for a 3-cylinder 2-8-0 compared with the 2-cylinder version, but these were hardly sufficiently wide-ranging to provide categorical proof one way or the other, nor were they repeated at increasing locomotive mileages. Whether the 'B17s', the 'D49s', or the 'V1/V3' tanks would or would not have been better locomotives with only two cylinders will never be known. The only comparative evidence was produced after Thompson had begun to rebuild the

'B17s' with 225lb/sq in boilers and two 20in×26in cylinders. From such tests as took place, the original, unconverted, locomotives seemed to have a slight edge. No figures were ever produced by Thompson to justify his rebuilding of examples of other classes from three to two cylinders. However, in the discussion which followed Spencer's Paper on the Development of LNER Design at the Institution of Locomotive Engineers in 1947, Cox commented that Gresley's 3-cylinder policy was inconsistent, and basing his argument on comparisons between LMS 2- and 3-cylinder 2-6-4Ts, found it difficult to accept the reasons for three cylinders in small and medium power locomotives. This was not an unreasonable approach: why provide more cylinders when two will do the job? The fact remains that Gresley believed that three would do the job better.

Gresley of course was not the only CME to have adopted a 3-cylinder layout, but he was alone in applying it systematically to a series of locomotives. Maunsell, no doubt following Holcroft's advice, applied it to mixed traffic 2-6-0s, initially in 1922, with, moreover, derived motion for the inside valves. A contributory reason may have been that these were intended for the Hastings line, with its reduced clearances; he built otherwise identical engines with two cylinders. Certainly this consideration lay behind the adoption of three cylinders in his outstanding 'Schools' class of 4-4-0. Bulleid followed suit in his 4-6-2s, no doubt for the same reasons as Gresley, as with the high boiler pressure of his engines he might otherwise have got away with a 2-cylinder design. On the LMS, the 'Royal Scots', the 'Patriots' and some 2-6-4Ts also had three cylinders, as well as, surprisingly, Stanier's 'Jubilees'. That the 'Jubilees', the LMS equivalent of the 'Castles' should have had three cylinders adds a piquancy to the debate over the non-appearance of an LNER 'Castle', never to mature, and eventually to be ousted from the scene by the 'V2'.

One subsidiary consequence of Gresley's 3-cylinder designs was his inability to produce a satisfactory and sufficiently stiff big-end for his larger locomotives. Originally a marine pattern, improved by Harrison by the introduction of a cotter type, and again by Cook, following the Swindon pattern, it was later felt that the solution lay in a well fitted bearing, adequately lubricated, and kept really tight.

Two other multi-cylinder projects may be mentioned. A six-cylinder version of the 'D49' was seriously considered in 1929, the engine being of 'vee' formation, with twin crankshafts, the drive being transmitted through bevel gearing and a jackshaft, whilst in 1939 similar preliminary ideas were explored for a six-coupled design, with the gears enclosed in an oil bath.

Gresley's attitude towards the compound use of steam was almost wholly negative, and only in the 4-6-4 No 10000 did he try this out in practice. As the boiler of the 'Hush-hush' was based on marine practice, it was reasonable to follow this with a compound cylinder arrangement. However 10000 was a venture into the unknown so far as locomotive design was concerned, and whether it would have performed better as a 3-cylinder Pacific, as, it is believed, Gresley originally intended, is impossible to tell. Stamer is reported to have said that when 'D49' design was under preparation at Darlington in 1926, proposals were made for two to be built as compounds on the Smith-Deeley system, on the lines of the Midland Compounds then being constructed for the LMS. Perhaps compounding of No 10000 and of the 'Shires' was discussed at the same time. Indeed, it may have been Stamer himself who put forward the suggestion. After all, he had been on the North Eastern when W. M. Smith applied his compound system to a 4-4-0 in 1898, and, in a 4-cylinder version, to two 4-4-2s in 1906. Gresley did not rebuild these as simple engines, nor did he make any radical alterations to the four compound 4-4-2s built by Robinson in 1905/6, all of which continued in their compound form until withdrawal. Of the three examples built for the Great Northern, No 3292 was withdrawn in 1927, still as a compound, whilst the 'Vulcan' No 4300 was converted to simple working in 1917 with two 20in×26in outside cylinders driving on to the leading coupled wheels and No 4421 was rebuilt in 1921 as a standard Atlantic. Despite — or perhaps because of? — his original training at Crewe, Gresley did not appear disposed to follow any of Webb's ideas on compounding.

Of all the inside cylinder engines which appeared during Gresley's entire period in charge of locomotive design, only the J38/J39 was completely his own. Apart from the various classes built for the LNER almost entirely to the pre-grouping specifications, such as the 'D11s' and 'B12s', his 'J50' and 'N2' tank engines were derived from Ivatt, Gresley adding his own refinements to bring them up-to-date, whilst his GNR 0-6-0s were almost pure Ivatt. As an example of economy in designer's time, this policy must be applauded: in the lights of the period, the designs were adequate, and until diesel multiple units took over the Kings Cross suburban traffic from the 'N2s' and BR diesel-electric shunters replaced the 'J50s', these classes continued on the work for which they had been introduced 40 or more years earlier.

By the time Gresley was appointed Locomotive Engineer of the GNR in 1911, the advantages of piston valves over slide valves had become generally accepted, whilst a number of engineers had applied the valve gear developed by the Belgian, Walschaerts, as an improvement on the traditional Stephenson gear. Gresley followed suit, but kept well in touch with later developments in valve design, and the relevant operating gear. The use of poppet valves in the internal combustion engine led locomotive engineers to consider their application to the steam engine, and in the later days of the GNR, Bulleid was asked to investigate their possibilities. However the first practical example of LNER interest was the fitting in 1925 of horizontally mounted Lentz poppet valves to a Great Eastern 'J20' 0-6-0, No 8280, the valves being operated by oscillating cams and driven by conventional Stephenson gear. Application of poppet valves to this one engine was evidently to obtain information and experience in service; no further freight engines were so fitted, and No 8280 reverted to piston valves in 1937. However there must have been some satisfactory first impressions, as in 1926 similar valves were fitted to No 8516 of the 'B12' class, the passenger equivalent of the 'J20'. The 10 'B12s' built new in 1928 were also fitted with Lentz valves, and five more were converted between 1928 and 1930.

Concurrently with this work at Stratford, Darlington applied Lentz valves to six new 'Shires', Class D49/3, the drive being obtained from the normal Walschaerts gear plus a modification of the usual derived motion for the inside cylinder. Whilst the poppet valves themselves appeared to have performed satisfactorily, it was felt that better results would be obtained if the operating cams could be of a continuously rotating, rather than an oscillating, pattern, and a design was developed for a rotating cam. This was built into two of the class turned out in 1929, and in subsequent batches constructed in 1932-35, classed

D49/2 and named after 'Hunts'. Despite the incorporation of bevel gears into the drive, the rotating system functioned well mechanically, replacing the Walschaerts gear, but because the cam provided only five cut-off positions, there was insufficient variability in cut-off to permit optimum performance, and a later version provided seven positions. In all, 42 locomotives were turned out new with rotary cams and eventually all had the seven position cut-off control, whilst the six which had oscillating gear were converted to piston valve operation when their cylinders were renewed in 1938. As a further trial in the mid-1930s, two 'C7' Atlantics, Nos 732 and 2212, were altered to incorporate Lentz valves.

In contrast to the locomotives provided with poppet valves up to 1934, mainly engaged in secondary duties, and despite the lack of conclusive evidence as to their effectiveness in service, Gresley took the bold step of fitting Lentz valves to his 'P2' *Cock o' the North*, intended for high power output in arduous conditions, but this was his final application of this device to a new design. The later 'P2s' were built with piston valves and No 2001 was converted after only three years in its original form.

In other experiments, two 'D49/2s', Nos 282 and 365, were provided with an infinitely variable cut-off control, the first by redesign of the camshaft, and the second by substitution of steam pressure for springs to seat the valves. The gear on No 365 was removed in 1941, and the locomotive was rebuilt by Thompson with two inside cylinders as a prototype for a possible standard 4-4-0. The gear was stored, and in 1949, in one of the few BR inspired experiments on a pre-nationalisation locomotive, it was fitted to another 'D49', BR No 62764 (LNER No 361) but with springs to seat the valves. In retrospect, the extended application of Lentz poppet valves does not appear to have been greatly successful. The 'B12s' soon reverted to piston valves, and whilst the poppet valve 'D49s' continued their normal duties reasonably satisfactorily, such evidence as was available from comparative testing indicated that the advantage lay with the piston valve engines.

Still persisting with poppet valves, but employing the Caprotti system with vertically mounted valves, and achieving a fully variable cut-off, which had been tried on LMS 'Claughton' 4-6-0s, two of Robinson's largest passenger class were converted to poppet valves in 1929. These were Class B3, Nos 6166/68, having four cylinders and Stephenson motion, and were reputed to be heavy on coal, some economy being recorded after fitting with Caprotti valves. Gresley's original request was for the conversion of four, but the Board was deterred by the price of £950 per set of gear, and only authorised two. However in 1938/9 another two, Nos 6164/7, were converted, this time employing a modified form of Caprotti gear in which steam pressure was utilised instead of springs to return the valves to their seats. It was this form of Caprotti gear which was to be employed in later years on Class 5 4-6-0s for the LMS and British Railways, and on the *Duke of Gloucester*. The more positive valve movements provided by this type of gear were claimed to result in better use of steam and a sharper exhaust.

In addition to these specific experiments with novel forms of valves, steps were taken in LNER days to redesign the valve operations of certain pre-grouping classes. The most notable was the improvement in performance of the original 'A1' Pacifics, following a major revision of the valve gear. Gresley, somewhat unwillingly by all accounts, had been considering fitting longer travel valves to these locomotives from about 1924, and in this he was given some impetus by the superior performance of the 'Castles' in the 1925 exchanges. Later evidence was to indicate that the improved design of valve gear contributed far more to the 'Castles' superiority than did their higher boiler pressure; between 1927 and 1931 all the 'A1s' were converted to long travel valves, but most had to wait several years before they received 220lb boilers. At the other end of the passenger engine scale, 'N7' 0-6-2Ts built from July 1927 had longer valve travel than was provided for their predecessors, and earlier examples of the class were later brought to this standard. Under Thompson, as Mechanical Engineer, Stratford, in the early 1930s, extensive rebuilding of the 'Claud Hamilton' 4-4-0s included the substitution of piston for slide valves, and a major reconstruction of the 'B12' 4-6-0s involved the provision of longer travel valves. Finally, after Thompson had moved to Darlington, some modernisation of North Eastern 'D20' 4-4-0s included fitting larger diameter, longer travel, valves, but only four of the class were altered. The results of all these alterations indicate that the performance of a locomotive depended more than is often realised on factors not usually provided in tables of leading dimensions. Clearly, too, it paid to get the valve gear design right first time, when the locomotive was built. It was an expensive business to manufacture and fit new valve gear, so this step was generally only taken when major renewals were needed anyway.

Little consideration seems to have been given before the 1920s to the fact that once the steam has done its work in the cylinder it should be enabled to escape to the atmosphere freely, with the least possible obstruction. A Finn, Kylala, drew attention to the subject in 1919, and his ideas were taken up by the eminent French engineer, André Chapelon, in the Kylchap exhaust system introduced in 1926. This consisted essentially of a series of cowls, fitted beneath the chimney, with the effect of aiding the expulsion of exhaust gases and steam, so minimising back pressure and enabling better use to be made of the steam in the cylinders. For larger locomotives, Chapelon recommended the employment of two such systems exhausting through a double chimney. Bulleid, and later Gresley himself, became closely acquainted with Chapelon, and in 1928 arrangements were made for two 'D49s' to be equipped with single chimney Kylchap systems. However, this experiment did not appear to have been successful, possibly because of objections by the running staff that the cowls impeded tube cleaning operations.

When, early in the 1930s, Gresley was preoccupied with No 10000, he sought Chapelon's advice on possible improvements in the draughting system; this led to the provision of a twin exhaust arrangement. Also, a Kylchap double chimney system was fitted to each of the 'P2s' and in 1937 to an 'A3', No 2751, whilst the full benefit was realised in 1938 when No 4468 and three other 'A4s' were similarly fitted. It was reckoned in Gresley's office that this was the single most important factor in *Mallard's* performance in achieving 11mph more than the LMS 'Duchess', when a speed of 125mph was recorded over a distance of 300yd in 1938; at such high speeds, the LMS exhaust system was less able to provide a sufficiently free outlet for the volume of gases and steam exhausted. Wartime conditions precluded any further application of the Kylchap system, but the performance of the 'A3s' and 'A4s' was still further improved when the two classes were fitted with Kylchap exhausts and double chimneys in the 1950s.

Alone amongst British locomotive engineers, Gresley was sufficiently attracted by the 'booster', an American development which provided supplementary power when needed, to try it out in practice. By 1918 the increasing loadings of the long distance Great Northern expresses were beginning to exceed the capabilities of the Ivatt Atlantics, improved though many of them were through the refinements of superheating and piston valves. The main problems were in starting heavy trains, and in climbing the long 1 in 200 banks, and the idea occurred to Gresley that the Atlantics could benefit from being fitted with a booster engine driving the trailing wheels, and which could be cut in and out at will, so providing additional power when needed. But due to delays it was not until 1923 that No 4419 was fitted with a booster, with two 10in×12in cylinders, increasing the theoretical tractive effort by half from 17,450 to 25,950lb. The booster certainly helped the Atlantic to start more easily with a heavy load, but it soon drained the boiler of steam, and the trailing wheels tended to slip badly, so that the full benefit of the increased tractive effort could not be realised. Moreover the heavy unsprung weight at the back of the locomotive led to considerable oscillation when running, whilst leaking steam pipes added to the crews' discomfort by filling the cab with steam. Despite later modifications, the conversion cannot be said to have been a success, which makes it all the more surprising that the experiment should have been repeated several years later, this time with two of Raven's Atlantics, 'C7s' Nos 727 and 2171, which appeared in modified form in 1932. In this more radical conversion, a larger boiler was provided, and to give a better ride the locomotive was articulated to the tender, resulting in a 4-4-4-4 wheel arrangement. (Despite this, the 4-4-2 classification was retained, the conversions becoming Class C9). Hopes of giving the 'C7s' a new lease of life, and so providing more effective support to the Pacifics in the north-east, did not mature. An insoluble problem was presented by the inability of the mechanism to switch the booster in at a speed greater than 27mph, so that an express train had to be going slowly for the booster to be of use, and even up Cockburnspath speed did not often fall below 30-35mph.

Going back in time, Gresley's two 'P1' Mikados, his freight equivalent of the Pacifics, were fitted with boosters from new. Whether this was his original intention is not clear, but when the costings were completed it emerged that the locomotives had cost considerably more than the estimate, so the probability is that the boosters were an afterthought. However, even without the boosters the locomotives were too powerful for the work available for them, and the booster assembly was plagued with mechanical troubles, including fracture of the casting forming the manifold connection for the steam pipes, a weakness accentuated by the necessity to turn on a sharply curved triangle, as at that time New England did not possess a turntable capable of handling the Midakos. A final application of the booster was more successful, the locomotives concerned being the Robinson 0-8-4Ts, Class S1, used for hump shunting. In favourable circumstances the booster-assisted engines were able to propel 1,100tons up the hump, compared with only 750tons for unfitted members of the class.

Chapter 12

Locomotive Design: Structure and Ancillaries

Locomotives, once built, become worn, and have to be repaired, and components replaced, to keep them in running order. In this, they may be compared with the human body, in which the constituents are in a perpetual state of gradual change. Over a period of years the body undergoes a complete metamorphosis, but its owner's identity remains: he is still Charlie Smith, or whatever. Something similar occurs over the life of a locomotive. Bearings, joints and tyres wear out, boilers and steam pipes develop leaks, and frames crack; all need repair or replacement. Indeed, as the locomotive advances with age, repair gives way to replacement, even of major components, and by the time withdrawal takes place there may be little left of the original, although to the observer, outwardly it may seem to be unchanged. Moreover, few locomotives escaped alterations to the running numbers given when they were new — many LNER engines had their numbers changed at least three times, whilst some even had their names changed. But still the locomotive retained its identity in the records of the railway, and in the notebooks of the enthusiasts. *Flying Scotsman* today preserves the aura of *Flying Scotsman* of 1923, although probably little more than the cab and the wheel centres remain of the original, and there must be doubt about even these.

In one of the many sagacious remarks recalled by his contemporaries, Gresley informed the Institution of Locomotive Engineers that 'American engines are built to wear out; British engines are built to last.' There is no question that this applied to his own designs. No other modern British express class lasted as long in front line service as his original Pacifics. Benefitting from regular attention and modernisation, they were still hard at work on the East Coast route 35 years after their introduction to these duties; but this was only achieved by continual attention to the structure and the fabric of the locomotive before deterioration had gone too far. Even the neglect of the war years was corrected eventually, and the Gresley Pacifics enjoyed an Indian Summer during the 1950s.

A central feature of conventional British steam locomotive design were the main frames, cut from mild steel plate, generally $1\frac{1}{8}$in thick, to which the hornblocks and cylinders were fitted, and which in the smokebox, boiler and cab carried most of the weight of the locomotive. Designed and constructed as cold and stationary, this was the reverse of their condition in service, suffering uneven expansion and contraction, whilst the whole structure was subjected to the reciprocating thrust of the pistons and to twisting movement as the locomotive ran over undulations in the track and around curves. Frames could be assembled in too rigid a fashion, so that they tended to crack under stress, or at the other extreme if too flexible, tolerances became excessive and wear in the bearings of wheel and rods was accelerated. Heavy frames of course were an aid to adhesion, unless the designer was endeavouring to reduce weight to keep within a given maximum axle loading, when lightening apertures would be cut where stresses were thought to be least. Stiffening plates might be welded on at points of maximum stress. Nevertheless, the art of designing plate frames for steam locomotives was never really mastered, as the imponderables were too many and too great for contemporary methods of calculation.

The 'A3s' were an interesting case as frame cracking was a problem from their earliest days. Various modifications were introduced to overcome the difficulties, but by the end of their lives a large number had received replacement frames, often the front portion only as the rear end gave little trouble of this nature. The lessons learned were applied in the 'A4s', which had circular lightening holes, and increased radii at the top of the horn gaps, with all corners well rounded. Very few cases of cracked frames occurred in the 'A4s', but the same did could not be said of Thompson classes.

Boilers and fireboxes also had a limited life, and these would be repaired or replaced as their condition warranted. A locomotive might expect to have a number of different boilers in the course of a lifetime, each, after repair and overhaul, being taken into stock and made available if needed by the next engine due for repairs. The time would come, of course, when boilers had to be scrapped, and replacements manufactured.

Up to the time of World War 1, British locomotives were universally noted for their clean lines; designers went to great trouble to hide as much of the mechanism and as many of the appendages as possible under the boiler cladding or between the frames. Gresley was one of the first to bring the valve mechanism into the open, and by raising the running plate, exposing the wheels, but nevertheless he still contrived to maintain the British tradition of uncluttered lines as far as possible. But when, following his desire to search all avenues in efforts to reduce fuel consumption, he experimented with feed water heaters, the volume of the hardware associated with these encumbrances precluded any substantial concealment. Using exhaust steam, containing a substantial quantity of both latent and sensible heat, to raise the temperature of the water fed into the boiler is an obvious area for experimentation: difficulties arise in providing an effective heat exchanger which does not rapidly scale up in hard water areas, and in the general necessity for a pump for the feed water. His first trials were on the Great Northern where he experimented with an elementary system on a small number of locomotives which were distinguished by an elongated dome containing a small feed water reservoir. These trials were discontinued after a short period. Next, in 1922 he applied the Worthington system to 2-cylinder 2-8-0 GN No 476, and in 1925 the Dabeg system was tried on a 3-cylinder class '02' 2-8-0 No 3500. In 1927 an extensive range of trials was instituted, with 'C7' No 2163 being fitted with the Dabeg apparatus, and 'B12' No 8509 and 'C11' No 9903 with the Worthington system. That year also saw the commencement of a wide application of the French ACFI system, no fewer than 55 'B12s' being fitted with this over the next few years. 'C7s' Nos 728 and 2206 were similarly fitted, as well as Pacifics

Nos 2576 and 2580, and the pioneer 'P2', No 2001. In the last two instances it was possible to hide a fair proportion of the bulk of the water heater. But all of these attachments exhibited shortcomings in service, and were eventually removed after only a few years in some cases, except the Worthington system fitted to No 9903, which remained until the locomotive was withdrawn in 1937. It had become clear that the cost of maintaining the gear in good order outweighed the benefits obtained from fuel saving. Despite the theoretical advantages of pumped systems, it was later realised that the merits of the Davies and Metcalfe exhaust steam injector had not been sufficiently appreciated, and that worthwhile savings could be achieved with this device, at less initial cost. Eventually the Davies and Metcalfe injector was fitted on all main line locomotives, fuel savings of up to 5% being reported.

Drifting smoke and steam obscuring the driver's vision had been a problem since the early days of railways, but the difficulty was intensified with softer exhausts, shorter chimneys and higher speeds. The problem was tackled about the same time by the CMEs of the LMS, Southern, and LNER, the first two applying deflector sheets on either side of the smokebox; not particularly scientifically designed, but the exhaust was helped to clear the cab at the expense of the otherwise traditional lines of the locomotives. The situation was less acute on the Great Western since a rather more generous loading gauge and taper boilers with a downward sloping axis permitted a longer chimney than on other railways. Gresley's approach to the problem was characteristic: he was not going to have his engines disfigured by side sheets and either a neater solution would be found or the locomotive front would be redesigned. The 'Hush-hush' No 10000, the subject of so many innovations, was given an overall semi-streamlined outline, the precursor of later, improved, contours and instead of smoke deflectors as afterthoughts, the boiler cladding sheets were continued forward to shroud the smokebox front. This design was developed from experiments using powdered chalk in a wind tunnel, devised by Professor W. E. Dalby, of the City and Guilds Engineering College, whom Gresley consulted on scientific matters from time to time. Airflow was also aided by the provision of ducts leading from above the buffer beam to behind the chimney. The improvement in smoke lifting achieved with No 10000 was evidently reasonably satisfactory as the same outline was applied to the first two 'P2s', but without the ducts. Whilst some success was met with on No 2001, the softer exhaust of the piston valved No 2002 called for something more, and individual deflectors were added on each side of the smokebox. Later, more radical alterations to all three locomotives resulted in their receiving the wedge shaped fronts of the 'A4s'.

In the meantime, some experiments had been taking place with the Pacifics, Nos 2747 *Coronach* and 2751 *Humorist* being subjected to surgery at the smokebox top intended to encourage the lifting of smoke and exhaust steam clear of the boiler. After little more than a year No 2747 reverted to its original condition, but No 2751 suffered a series of experiments, including the first application to an 'A3' of a Kylchap exhaust and double chimney, the soft blast of which exacerbated the problem. Small deflector plates were fitted on each side of the chimney, and the locomotive remained in this condition for some years. Later CME's were less sensitive than Gresley to the appearance of large side sheets, and the Thompson and Peppercorn Pacifics received large LMS type deflectors, as did

Humorist in 1947. But when the 'A3s' as a class eventually were fitted with double exhaust pipes and chimneys, they were given trough type deflectors based on a German pattern, which had a more scientific derivation than simple side sheets, and which effectively solved the problem of obscured vision. This postwar development arose directly from the recommendation of P. N. Townend, the Kings Cross shedmaster at the time, who whilst in Germany took a photograph of a German DB Pacific fitted with these appendages, and arranged for Doncaster drawing office to design a type suitable for fitting to the 'A3s'. Whether the appearance of the class was improved or not depends upon one's viewpoint; where safety considerations are concerned, should not looks take second place?

Uncertainty about the best method of smoke lifting on the 'P2s' was resolved in a more fundamental way when Gresley took note of the wedge fronted Bugatti railcar running between Paris and Deauville. Some wind tunnel tests with 1/40th scale models at the National Physical Laboratory produced data on which the final shape was based, and although due to an error the contours followed in construction did not entirely accord with intention, the result was a satisfactory embodiment of streamlining as it was then understood, with a better-than-hoped-for achievement in smoke lifting. Streamlining, on the 'A4s' extended to fairings over the wheels, which improved the overall effect, but added to maintenance difficulties in that they had to be removed before access could be gained to the rods and motion. Labour had become so scarce by mid-1941 that T. C. B. Miller, then mechanical foreman at Haymarket, allowed one of his 'A4s' to visit Doncaster for overhaul without having replaced the skirting, which had been removed for minor attention to the motion. To his surprise, the locomotive was returned without comment from higher authority (he had expected a reprimand) and with curved insets fitted to soften the angles at the cylinders. This aid to maintenance had appealed to Thompson, now the CME, who gave instructions that all the 'A4s' should be given this treatment. A valuable bonus was that there was an improvement in air circulation, leading to cooler conditions in the inside mechanism, although there was a greater opportunity for dust and grit to enter. Two other locomotives were given streamlined bodywork in 1937; these were 'B17s' Nos 2859 and 2870, but in this case the treatment was purely cosmetic. These two, renamed *East Anglian* and *City of London* respectively, were intended to work the 'East Anglian' express, but the coaches were not streamlined, nor were the speeds achieved sufficiently high to gain much advantage from streamlining. The overall casing was removed in 1951. In 1936 it was reported that streamlining might be extended to one of the Ivatt Atlantics, but although a drawing was made for Gresley's consideration, it is unlikely that this was ever a serious proposal.

It was believed in postwar days that the new 6ft 8in class of Pacific was to be streamlined, and indeed outline drawings were made. But the vogue had passed, and apart from the 'air-smoothed' casing of the Pacifics which Bulleid continued to build for the Southern Railway, nothing more was seen in Britain; indeed, the LMS removed the streamlining from those members of the 'Coronation' class which had borne this. With the rebuilding of the 'P2s' into Pacifics, and the removal of the casing from the two 'B17s', the 'A4s' and the rebuilt 'W1' remained the only examples of streamlined locomotives.

The Great Northern was not a pioneer in lessening the enginemen's discomfort by providing more commodious cabs; in fact as late as 1920 the projected Pacific still possessed nothing more than a larger version of the cutout cabside type of the early Ivatt days, and which had been the pattern at Doncaster ever since. However, B. Spencer, then a draughtsman at Doncaster, was set to work on an outline more in keeping with contemporary practice, and based on the Great Eastern side window pattern, first introduced on 'Claud Hamilton' at the turn of the century. Gresley was impressed by this, as with Spencer's layout of the cab; the outcome was the application of variants of the basic design to all Gresley's subsequent tender engines, and to Spencer's promotion to a position in the CME's office. In a later revision, this time following practice on the PLM Railway in France, a wedge shaped spectacle plate was introduced, giving the advantage of a clearer, less reflecting, view forward. First applied to the 'P2s', and later to the 'A4s' and 'V2s', this feature was discarded by Thompson but restored in modified form to the Peppercorn Pacifics.

Ivatt's Atlantics were reputed to give their crews a rough ride, despite the trailing wheels, which might have afforded some relief. Gresley's wide firebox classes on the other hand usually gave a relatively smooth ride, attributed to improvements in springing generally, and to the damping effect of the Cartazzi slides controlling the trailing wheels. An appreciative letter from an anonymous LMS fireman would have warmed Gresley's heart. Soon after nationalisation he had a ride on a Pacific for the first time and wrote to say he 'thought he was sitting inside a first class coach compared with the Black Fives to which he was accustomed.' Yet in contrast the 'B17s', 'D49s' and 'K3s' all suffered from hard riding at speed. The reason for this is unclear; after all, the problem did not appear to exist on the Great Western 'Kings' and 'Castles', whilst the three cylinder arrangement should have helped matters. Probably the answer lay in the springing, an area in which scientifically produced design information was lacking owing to the difficulty of taking accurate measurements on a locomotive in service, trial and error providing the only basis for improvement. If the locomotive was in a rundown condition, cylinder output tended to be uneven, adding to the movement transmitted to the cab, whilst the design and performance of the pony truck or bogie would also contribute to the quality of riding. Following Ivatt's practice, Gresley favoured a system of swing links to control sideways movement, and which in theory tended to equalise the weight on the leading wheels when rounding curves, but they permitted excessive lateral play when worn, and there was also difficulty of access for maintenance. Derailments of two 'V2s' in 1946 were attributed primarily to faulty track, but the swing link system came in for some criticism and steps were taken to change to a more conventional type of spring side control. Gresley had in fact already reviewed bogie design when the 'D49s' first appeared, after which links were discarded on bogies and replaced by spring control, but the 'V2s' and other designs incorporating a pony truck continued to employ the swing link system until after the war.

Not perhaps an aspect of locomotive design as such, but an important factor in the costs of boiler maintenance, was the nature of the feed water. Gresley appreciated the advantages which would accrue if all his locomotives could be supplied with water of zero hardness, but realised that this would be a costly business, involving considerable investment in water treatment plant, particularly for water softening. The first thing to do was to establish the composition of the many feed water sources on the LNER system, so that appropriate chemical treatment could be devised. This problem was tackled by T. Henry Turner, the LNER Chief Chemist and Metallurgist, and his team of chemists in the Areas, who after detailed investigation drew up a list of sources to be treated, and sites for plant. The first part of the system to be tackled was the Great Northern main line, with the result that when *Mallard* made its record breaking run, zero hardness water was supplied to its boiler. Although the other main line railways were naturally concerned about the quality of their feed water, none was as far advanced as the LNER in knowledge of the composition of their sources, an essential pre-requisite to the corrective treatment. The work of the LNER team, inspired by Gresley, led to standardised approaches to the whole question of water treatment for boilers, both for land and marine use.

Whilst on the Great Northern, Gresley had done little to alter traditional 6-wheeled tender design as handed down from Stirling and Ivatt, and even his initial Pacific projection had a similar pattern of tender. He later considered that a larger tender should be provided, with greater coal and water capacity, and so whilst following the earlier designs with a plain profile and coal rails, an eight-wheeled version was developed and accompanied No 1470 when it appeared in 1922. A new design of six-wheeled tender was drawn up at Darlington, soon after grouping, and this first appeared with the third locomotive of the large order for 'K3s' turned out at Darlington, the first Gresley class to be built there. Water capacity was 4,200gal, coal 7½tons, and this tender represented the most wide ranging application of standardisation in the LNER locomotive fleet, continuing to be built up to the end of 'B1' construction in 1952, by which time over a thousand had been constructed. Originally distinguished by stepped out copings, the appearance was later altered by the provision of flush sides, whilst other detailed amendments were made from time to time. A variation introduced in 1926 was smaller and lighter, with water capacity 3,500gal and coal 5½ton; these were coupled to locomotives such as the 'J38s', engaged on short hauls without the need for water pickup.

Gresley's design instructions for the new Group Standard tender were straightforward. Outlining his ideas in blue pencil on a contemporary North Eastern drawing, he told R. J. Robson, then Chief Draughtsman at the Locomotive Drawing Office at Darlington, that he wanted a coal cart, not a hearse.

A unique innovation in tender design appeared in 1928 in the form of a corridor version of the GNR eight-wheeled type, introduced to allow crews to be changed on the non-stop 'Flying Scotsman' between Kings Cross and Edinburgh. The tender outline was improved in appearance, with the side sheets reaching as high as the cab roof, and with water capacity increased to 5,000gal, and coal to as much as 9ton. A similar, non-corridor, type was introduced with the 1930 batch of 'A3s' and this tender, with minor modifications, continued to be built for the 'P2s' and the postwar Pacifics as well. Corridor tenders were exchanged from time to time between engines, but when all 35 'A4s' were in service the corridor tenders — 22 in all — were kept with selected locomotives of this class. Other locomotives exchanged tenders on occasion, according to the work on which they were engaged, but generally the new Group Standard tenders were not associated with pre-grouping locomotives, although several instances may be quoted of newly built engines being provided with pre-grouping tenders, sometimes from withdrawn locomotives, to save the cost of contructing new tenders. In addition to the Group Standard tenders, the short Great Eastern pattern tender was also built for the 1928 batch of 'B12s', as well as the 'B17s' named after country estates. The 'B17s' were not provided with standard tenders until the 'Footballers' emerged in 1936, after length restrictions had been relaxed.

Practically all Nigel Gresley's locomotives — and with certain obvious exceptions those of his LNER successors too — displayed certain family characteristics. There was a harmony of line which seemed to accommodate the obtrusions of boiler mountings and the hardware associated with outside cylinders. The traditional flat running plate, level from front buffer beam to end of tender, often with deep splashers to allow for driving wheels and coupling rods, was discarded on almost all his designs in favour of a gently curving raised running plate which exposed the whole of the wheels of all but his largest wheeled engines, for which small splashers were provided. A form of 'S' curve for the running plate was featured on most outside cylindered locomotives; this had its origins as far back as Stirling's Singles, and was continued by Ivatt on his Atlantics. A variation on the continuous curve of the running plate was the quadrant introduced by Raven on certain North Eastern engines, and which came through on the 'J38', 'J39' and 'D49' Darlington designs, and strangely on the 'V1' tanks. Thompson, perhaps to stamp his own productions in a slightly different way to Gresley, favoured the quadrant, with an even higher, straight, running plate.

A final commentary may perhaps be offered on chimneys, often considered an important feature of a locomotive's identity, but becoming increasingly less conspicuous as boilers grew larger and mountings were cut down to the LNER Composite Load Gauge. Chimneys for Gresley's new designs were neat and excited no particular comment, but his standard replacements on pre-grouping locomotives were criticised for showing lack of sympathy with the original design, particularly Robinson's, on which the original chimneys of an elegant Edwardian style were replaced by a very functional type dubbed the 'flowerpot'. During the experiments to discover a way to improve methods of lifting the exhaust of the Pacifics, No 2751 carried a rimless chimeny, as did the postwar Pacifics when they first arrived. These were later replaced by a lipped pattern, but none of the streamlined locomotives were ever provided with anything other than a rimless casing to the exhuast outlet. One experiment which owed nothing to the Gresley influence was seen when K. J. Cook fitted a Swindon copper cap to a 'V2', BR No 60854. Few observers had the opportunity of judging whether or not the engine's appearance was improved or not, but Spencer for one thought it looked quite good. However, word of the embellishment soon reached R. A. Riddles, then responsible for all BR rolling stock, and word was sent down the line without delay. 'Take it off', Cook was told, 'This could be regarded as an act of aggression.'

This brief and discursive summary of the main components of Gresley's influence on locomotive design necessarily omits his many less spectacular developments — on lubrication systems, for example, on axleboxes, regulator patterns and other details. He was always on the lookout for some device to improve efficiency and to apply it experimentally to one or two of his locomotives, particularly the large ones. The 'A1' and 'A3' Pacifics were especially vulnerable to some minor piece of gadgetry, so much so that it has been said that on occasion no two members of these classes were exactly alike.

As to Gresley's own view on his influence on locomotive design, Kaye McCosh, the son of Andrew K. McCosh, who for many years was Chairman of the LNER Locomotive Committee, recalled Gresley visiting his father at his estate in Lanarkshire. As a schoolboy, Kaye McCosh was introduced to Gresley and asked him what he considered to be his greatest contribution to steam locomotive practice. The reply was straightforward. 'Streamlining the steam passages', said Gresley. Indeed, on the 'A4s', when working with short cut-off and full regulator, there was practically no pressure drop between the boiler and the cylinder.

Above: Class O4/8 No 6590, reboilered with
round topped firebox, side window cab,
and GN chimney. Peterborough, June
1946. *Wethersett Collection/IAL*

Below: BR No 63773, rebuilt by Thompson
as Class O1, at Acton, Western Region, on
South Wales freight train during 1948 loco
exchanges. *C. C. B. Herbert*

Above: No 2394 booster fitted 'P1' on up coal train at Potters Bar, March 1929. *Wethersett Collection/IAL*

Right: No 3571, Class J6, built at Doncaster in 1913. *L&GRP, courtesy David & Charles*

Below: No 3602, Class J6 on up goods at Trumpington, June 1932. *Wethersett Collection/IAL*

Above: No 5919 (1946 renumbering), Class J38 at Prestonpans, April 1948. *Wethersett Collection/IAL*

Right: No 2991, Class J39, on fast GE Section working. *Real Photos*

Below: No 4650 (1946 renumbering), Gresley rebuild of 'J19' at Ipswich, May 1948. *Wethersett Collection/IAL*

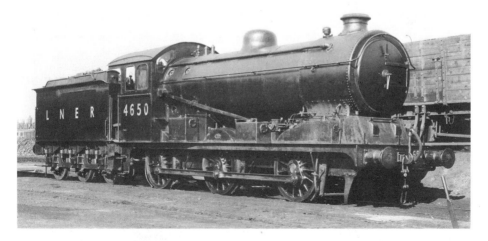

Top: No 9499 (1946 renumbering) 'N2' with GN Section quad-art sets on down Welwyn Garden City Train, at New Southgate, August 1948. *Wethersett Collection/IAL*

Above: BR No 62060, Peppercorn Class K1 at York, October 1964. *Brian Stephenson*

Below: No 2943, Class J39, at Nottingham Victoria with an up excursion train formed of London suburban quad-arts. *T. G. Hepburn/Rail Archive Stephenson*

Above: BR No 69490, 'N2' with GN quad-art sets on up Hatfield train near Potters Bar, May 1951. *Brian Morrison*

Left: GN No 1766, Class N2, built by NBL in passenger green livery. *IAL*

Below: BR No 69538, still coping with GN suburban traffic after almost 40 years at Kings Cross. *IAL*

Above: No 1771 Robinson Class A5, built by Hawthorn Leslie in 1926 for North Eastern Area. *Real Photos*

Left: No 2643, Class N7, in original LNER form. *Real Photos*

Below: BR No 69701, rebuilt 'N7' with round topped firebox. Stratford, April 1960. *Wethersett Collection/IAL*

Above: No 2906, one of the first batch of 'V1s', built at Doncaster 1930. *Real Photos*

Right: Photomontage prepared on Thompson's instructions purporting to illustrate his proposed 'L1' 2-6-4T. Prepared by adding longer tanks, larger bunker and trailing bogie to a photo of a 'V1'. *Crown Copyright, National Railway Museum, York.*

Below: No 9000, prototype of Thompson's 'L1' class. Gateshead in July 1946. *Wethersett Collection/IAL*

Above, top to bottom: *Flower of Yarrow*,
100 hp Sentinel steam railcar. *Crown
Copyright, National Railway Museum, York*

Northumbrian, Armstrong Whitworth
diesel railcar. *Crown Copyright, National
Railway Museum, York*

Class J50 No 585 at Kings Cross, August
1939. *Wethersett Collection/IAL*

No 9999 (1946 renumbering), Class U1
2-8-0 + 0-8-2 Garratt at Mexborough, May
1948. *Wethersett Collection/IAL*

Above: Class J72, No 8680 (1946
renumbering) built at Darlington 1899.
Employed in carriage shunting at
Newcastle, August 1947. Specially painted
in fully lined-out green livery, sans serif
characters. *Wethersett Collection/IAL*

Right: Sentinel Class Y3, No 117, built 1931.
Real Photos

Below: Worsdell 4-8-0T Class T1 No
1658, built at Darlington 1925. Note typical
NER lineaments. *Crown Copyright,
National Railway Museum, York*

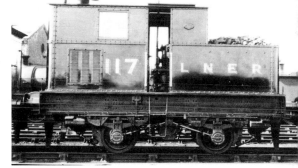

Right: Thompson 'Q1' rebuild No 9931.
Gateshead July 1946. *Wethersett
Collection/IAL*

Below right: Originally outlined by Gresley
as Class EM1, but built 10 years after his
death. No 76.016 seen here in rail blue with
BR number and logo at Guide Bridge,
September 1979. *B. J. Nicolle*

Below: No 732, Raven Atlantic modified
with poppet valves driven by rotating cam
mechanism, and with higher running plate.
Wethersett Collection/IAL

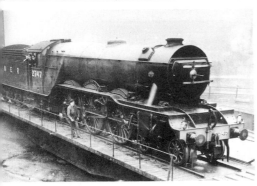

Top: Class B12 No 8560 with ACFI feed water heater, on up express at Littlebury, July 1933. *Wethersett Collection/IAL*

Above: Class B12 No 8520 with ACFI feedwater heater, at Whittlesfield, July 1932. *Wethersett Collection/IAL*

Left: No 2747 *Coronach* with cut-away smokebox. *Real Photos*

Above: BR No 60103 *Flying Scotsman* with trough-type smoke detectors and double chimney, at Kings Cross, January 1963. Seen just prior to last BR revenue earning trip to Doncaster. *BR*

Below: No 60100 *Spearmint* with trough-type smoke deflectors and double chimney, coming off the Forth Bridge with a Dundee-Edinburgh freight. *Dugald Cameron*

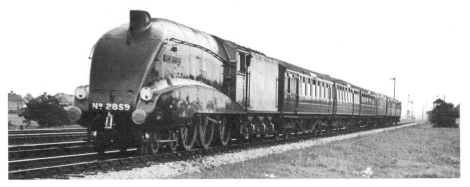

Top: No 2859 *East Anglian* in streamlined form. *Crown Copyright, National Railway Museum, York*

Above: No 2859 *East Anglian* seen in action on up 'East Anglian' at Chadwell Heath, June 1938. *Wethersett Collection/IAL*

Below: No 4486 *Merlin* disguised at No 1931 *Davina* in 1944. *Crown Copyright, National Railway Museum, York*

Above: Sir Nigel Gresley feeding mallards at Salisbury Hall. *Author's Collection*

Left: H.N. Gresley in his office in Great Northern Days. (Note pad at right of knee-hole to protect his injured leg). *Author's Collection*

Chapter 13

Locomotive Identification

A widely believed piece of railway mythology is that until labour shortages in the 1940s prevented proper maintenance, let alone cleaning, locomotives were invariably kept clean and shining. Well, the situation during the LNER period was certainly better than in the early days of British Railways, but it would be wrong to assume that every engine on the railway was always in pristine condition. I recall, in about 1928, a Pacific hauling a down express through Oakleigh Park which was so dirty that the number was quite indecipherable. Fortunately the nameplate was readable, so that the engine could be identified as *Dick Turpin*, then stationed at Heaton. Another sighting around this time was of a grubby 2-8-0 which bore in chalk the words 'LNER can't afford to pay for cleaning this engine'.

Because the steam engine inherently generates a great deal of smoke, dirt and cinders, keeping it clean is a never ending task, and it is more important that the inside, which isn't seen, should be kept clean, rather than the outside, which is. All credit is due to the anonymous crews of cleaners who so often took a pride in their work, and turned out their engines looking a credit to their shed, only to have to start again when their charges returned. Because of its dirty nature, the obvious choice of colour for a locomotive is matt black, so that the dirt shows less. Brightly coloured engines need a great deal of cleaning unless the expensive finish is to be neglected. Victorian and Edwardian engines in fact were almost all painted in cheerful colours, and much effort was expended on cleaning them. However the story is possibly apocryphal that William Stroudley of the LBSCR was in the habit of touching the smokeboxes of his 'Gladstone' engines with his forefinger — and if it came away dirty the driver was reprimanded. Matthew Stirling, of the Hull & Barnsley, was said to put his hand *behind* the spokes of driving wheels on his passenger engines.

When Nigel Gresley became Locomotive Engineer of the Great Northern in 1911, all the company's locomotives were painted apple green, with black lining edged with white, the tender sides outside the lining being a darker, olive, green. A great deal of work went into preparing, painting and varnishing whenever a locomotive was built or overhauled; several coats were applied, and the period a locomotive was out of traffic for the purpose could amount to as much as six weeks. Pride of workmanship put into the finish of the locomotive was reflected not only by the painter himself, but by those in the top management of the railway. Few people seem to have considered this an area for cost saving, although it is said that when Francis Webb of the LNWR was asked why he painted his engines black, he replied that he would paint them in gold leaf when the shareholders' dividends warranted it. However Webb's black was a shiny blackberry black, well lined out, and the only saving over a red or green alternative would have been the lower cost of the black paint.

Gresley had only been in office a year when in December 1912 he recommended to the Great Northern Board that goods and shunting engines should be painted grey in the interests of economy, and that he could save £1,000 a year by doing this; the Board agreed. The grey engines in fact looked very smart and photographed well. A neat white line edged the boiler bands and splashers, and enhanced the general effect. His next involvement in the colours of his locomotives was after the formation of the LNER, when the Board had to decide how to paint their fleet, choosing from pre-grouping colours of blue, brown, grey, black and four shades of green. Exhibitions were arranged at York and Marylebone, and after considering the alternatives the Locomotive Committee, then chaired by Bernard Firth, of the Great Northern, recommended to the Board that express passenger engines with driving wheels of 6ft 6in and over should be painted green, and others black; the shade of green to be that used by the GNR. This was endorsed by the Board, but the influence of William Whitelaw may be discerned in the added proviso that the NB 'Glen' class (with 6ft 0in wheels) should also be painted green.

The Board decision made no recommendation beyond the bare colours, matters of lining being left to the CME, who retained the Great Northern black/white lining for green engines, and introduced red lining from the North Eastern for those painted black. Some points were never codified, the works differing in detail, such as the colour applied to outside cylinder covers — black if painted at Doncaster, green if painted at Darlington.

The Board made two later decisions concerning the colour of locomotives. In May 1928, Gresley's recommendation was accepted that in the interests of economy, passenger engine green should be limited to 340 engines. These would include the Pacifics, the large Atlantics, and the large 4-6-0s on the GC and GE Sections. All other express engines were to be black, with a fine red line, goods engines black, given one coat of varnish only and left without lining. An annual saving of £13,000 was predicted. The last occasion on which the Board considered the question of livery was in July 1946, when one of Peppercorn's first moves was to obtain authority to paint all locomotives GN green, except the streamline passenger engines which were to be blue. The point was firmly recorded that there were to be no other exceptions unless specifically authorised. In retrospect, a fine declaration, but nothing was said about cleaning the locomotives once they had been painted.

In the event, neither of these two directives on livery was to be wholly obeyed. Gresley's 1928 proposals did not mention his 'D49' 4-4-0s, but these, and the two 'Royal Clauds' continued to be green. There was no Board authority in the 1930s for painting the 'A4s' silver, or blue, or (during the war) black, nor for Thompson's revival of Great Eastern blue for the first appearance of the rebuilt No 4470. A good deal of green paint was applied in 1946 and 1947, but the cheerful Great Northern green soon disappeared under a coating of grime. The later British Railways colours of course owed nothing to Gresley, but to some observers the Pacifics were not unpleasing in Great Western green.

Great Northern locomotives were lettered and numbered in block characters, beautifully shaded and very legible, a style which was retained by the LNER, except that the numbers were generally larger and affixed beneath the letters on tenders and tanksides. This meant that tenders could not be exchanged without renumbering, but the point was not taken until after the introduction of corridor tenders in 1928, which necessarily had to be attached to the Pacifics selected for non-stop running; numbers were then transferred to the cabsides. The practice at Doncaster and Darlington was to position the number below the cab window if possible, and to align the letters with it, even though this would often result in the 'LNER' being above the centre line of the tender; Gorton however did not follow this style at once, and for many years positioned the letters in the centre of the tender side.

When in 1932 the LNER standardised on Gill Sans lettering for all timetables, leaflets, notices and internal documents, both printed and painted, and made a conscious effort to present the public with a standardised house style, Gresley continued to use block characters on his locomotives, and broad Roman characters with elongated serifs on his coaching stock. With the introduction of the streamline trains in 1935 however, Gill Sans appeared on the new coaches, and later on, certain of the 'A4s' were given stainless steel cut out letters and numbers to match. When LNER locomotives were repainted after the war, and new numbers applied under the renumbering scheme, block characters were employed at first, but an unshaded sans serif style was soon brought in.

In pre-grouping discussions, the name of the new company, the London and North Eastern Railway, was not arrived at without controversy. A better title of course would have been 'Great Northern', because that described its main direction, but this would not have been acceptable to North Eastern interests. For a time, 'Great North Railway' was considered — after all, there was a Great North Road, and the East Coast main line followed its course, but in the end, 'L&NER' was adopted, the ampersand soon being omitted. Wagons were merely lettered 'NE' from the start, as were locomotives and coaches during the war.

Each of the constituent members of the LNER followed a system of locomotive numbering which allocated blocks of new numbers as the stock increased, as well as filling in gaps in the register as older engines were withdrawn. The Great Northern was a little more coherent than most of the others in that classes were numbered mainly, but by no means always, in blocks. Prior to grouping one of the first matters to engage the attention of the Mechanical Engineers was a system by which locomotives — and carriages and wagons — could be renumbered. At their first meeting after the formation of the LNER, in 1923, Gresley's suggestion was accepted that for the time being existing numbers should be retained, with the addition of suffix letters to indicate pre-grouping origin, and to differentiate between locomotives carrying the same numbers. In 1924, after he had become CME, block arrangements were decided upon, 3000 being added to Great Northern numbers, 5000 to Great Central, 6800 to Great North of Scotland, 7000 to Great Eastern and 9000 to North British. North Eastern engines retained their existing numbers unchanged, whilst Hull & Barnsley locomotives absorbed into the NER and previously renumbered in the 3000s were renumbered again between 2405 and 2542. After some initial disagreement a similar scheme was adopted for carriages and wagons, except that to save some cost in renumbering, and to aid number taking by checkers, an initial digit only was added to the pre-grouping number. In addition to new building the LNER locomotive stock was augmented when locomotives were absorbed from the M&GN Joint in 1936 and the London Passenger Transport Board in 1937. M&GN engines retained their number with the addition of a prefix 'O', whilst those of the LPTB were numbered into the Great Central block.

New locomotives built in 1923/4 to pre-grouping orders were numbered within the blocks allocated to their old companies, but with the commencement of deliveries of post-grouping orders, there was less coherence. Locomotives would either be numbered in the vacant spaces following the last Hull & Barnsley engine, commencing with the 40 Pacifics Nos 2543-2582, or inserted into vacancies in the North Eastern list. This was partly in deference to NE wishes that locomotives allocated to that area should bear numbers within the North Eastern block. The 60 'K3s' delivered from Darlington in 1924/5 for example occupied various numbers from 17 to 231, but numbers within this series were not kept for later 'K3s' as some of the 'D49s', commencing with 201, overlapped them. The only new class of any size to be numbered entirely consecutively were the 'B17s', which took 2800-72. The 'V1s' started off in good order from 2900, but did not progress beyond 2933, most later additions taking vacant numbers in the 300s and 400s.

Good use was made of the vacant space following the last Great Central number, 6252. The first batch of 125 'O4' 2-8-0s purchased from disposal sources, as a GC design naturally fell in place as 6253-6377, and they were followed by another GC revival, the 'D11s' built in 1924 for service in Scotland, which occupied the numbers 6378-6401. Locomotives on the GC duplicate list, previously identified by a suffix 'B' to their running numbers were renumbered 6402-94, and were followed by the remainder of the bought-in 'O4s' which took the block 6495-6642. However the Robinson 'A5s' built for the North Eastern were numbered in gaps in the 1700s, within the NER series. In Gresley's time no new locomotives were given numbers in the Great Eastern or the North British series, apart from deliveries in the first year or so after grouping, the 1928 batch of 'B12s', 8571-80, and the odd Sentinel shunting engine. The 'Hush-hush', No 10000, was the only new locomotive with a five digit number, although several locomotives on the NBR duplicate list were renumbered in the 10000s. (Strangely, the few Great Northern engines on the duplicate list were not renumbered at the time but retained their suffix 'A'.) As more new engines were built in the 1930's, blocks were taken in the Great Northern series, although originally the 'V2s' and the second batch of 'A4s' were to have received numbers which had become blank in the North Eastern series. 'V2' No 4771, for instance, was first numbered 637, and 'A4' No 4482 was to have been 2063. All this apparent confusion adds of course to the peculiar charm which is such a part of the Gresley scene.

The relative administrative benefits, if any, of numbering locomotives with little or no regard to sequence, of which system the LNWR was a leading exponent, or in blocks of a hundred, like the Great Western, or with a prefix denoting the class, as on most Continental railways and present day British Rail, cannot be gauged. In 1936 a number of alternative schemes were drawn up to bring LNER standard locomotives into consecutive blocks of numbers, but no action was taken. Overhaul of the numbering system had to wait until Thompson initiated an orderly system by renumbering the whole of the LNER locomotive stock according to a schedule, which after some interim renumbering to allow the new 'B1s' a clear and lengthy block from 8301 onwards, gave the lowest numbers to the most powerful passenger engines, apart from No 10000 which retained its five digits, and the highest numbers to the goods tank engines. As a different example of the Gresley influence, BR renumbering followed the system introduced by him after the grouping. After a brief interval during which prefix letters were applied to denote regional ownership, locomotives were allocated five digit blocks of numbers by the addition of 30000 to Southern, 40000 to LMS and 60000 to LNER running numbers. There were a few exceptions, one of the most notable being that 10000, which had escaped renumbering under the Thompson scheme, now became 60700. Great Western numbers were unchanged, and special blocks were allocated to diesel and electric locomotives.

A fine administrative distinction was observed on the LNER in that whilst the Chief Mechanical Engineer was responsible for painting, lettering and numbering locomotives, names were formally selected by the Chief General Manager and a list conveyed by memorandum to the CME, who arranged for the nameplates to be prepared. Nevertheless it is inconceivable that Gresley was unconcerned about the names given to his engines, and in all probability approved or even selected them before a formal memorandum was written. His career had spanned the LNWR, on which almost every express engine bore a name, often of some obscure character from mythology, through the Lancashire and Yorkshire, which possessed no named engines, to the Great Northern, which had one, the first Atlantic, named *Henry Oakley*, after the General Manager of the period. But with the first two Gresley Pacifics a new tradition began, and with grouping imminent *Great Northern* and *Sir Frederick Banbury* commemorated a railway and its chairman, soon to pass into history. After the grouping, more Pacifics were named, for particular reasons. Amongst these were *Flying Scotsman*, given to No 4472 as a Public Relations gesture in support of its appearance at the British Empire Exhibition in 1924; No 2563, named *William Whitelaw* in 1924, after the LNER Chairman; and *Centenary* was conferred on No 2555, the first Pacific to be completed in 1925, the year of the Stockton & Darlington Centenary.

But of course it was the racehorse names which appealed to so many of the public and the railway staff, although the decision to give the class the names of famous racehorses was not taken until some time after the Pacifics had begun to appear in quantity. The first racehorse name was seen in April 1925, when No 4475 was named *Flying Fox*. The names were an extraordinary selection, some splendid, like *Royal Lancer* and *Grand Parade*, others faintly absurd, such as *Spearmint* and *Sandwich*, or, like *Ladas* incomprehensible to the layman. There seemed to be no logic in the choice, they were not chosen in alphabetical or chronological order, not grouped by race or owner or jockey, not even chosen for their speed. There were horses and fillies, but they were all flat racers, not a hurdler amongst them. There were Derby and St Leger winners, winners of other classics and even minor races, but none of the Grand National. Whose brilliant idea it was to name the Gresley 'A1' and 'A3' Pacifics after racehorses may never be known, but it seems that there was no original intention to give them names, as a class. Indeed it may be fortuitous that apart from a handful of 'specials' they were named at all; certainly it was not originally intended to name them after racehorses. Neither William Whitelaw nor Nigel Gresley are known to have been greatly interested in the turf, nor was Sir Ralph Wedgwood, but in all probability some of the Board members had connections with racing circles. The fifth Lord Rosebery had been a director of the Great Northern, and four of his horses were commemorated by Pacifics, so there is a possibility that the inspiration for the naming came from the Board Room. Perhaps the directors were allowed to nominate their favourites, but it is known the Gresley kept a copy of a stud book in his office, and possibly in a relaxed moment picked out names which took his fancy. Despite an appearance of sternness to those who did not know him well, he possessed a whimsical sense of humour which would see no incongruity in names such as *Pretty Polly* or even *Hermit* for his Pacifics. Some enginemen believed that the horses were 'those which Gresley had a tanner on', but this, even if true on occasion, was an impossibility in many cases, particularly the oldest in time, a filly named *Blink Bonny*, which came home first in the Derby and Oaks as long ago as 1857, many years before Gresley was born. (She would have won the St Leger as well, had her jockey not 'pulled' her, causing a celebrated scandal at the time.)

When the 'A4s' were first seen, in their distinctive silver grey, perhaps it was William Whitelaw who recalled his Sir Walter Scott, as it is in 'The Lay of the Last Minstrel' that the lines appear 'True love's the gift which God has given .. the silver link . . . which heart and heart can bind'. Not wholly apposite, but taken out of context a splendid title to introduce the new class of locomotives. Most of the 'A4s' were given the names of species of birds, and these were certainly Gresley's own choice. He delighted in feeding the mallards at his home at the time, Salisbury Hall, near St Albans, and told his daughters that he would name one of his new engines *Mallard*. Indeed, A. E. Beresford, then on his staff at Kings Cross, recalls that one day he wrote a list of suitable names on a sheet of paper — *Falcon*, *Peregrine* and about a dozen others. In 1936, K. Risdon Prentice, who was then engaged with Peter Proud in producing the first comprehensive survey of LNER locomotives to be published, realised that the hundredth Pacific would be built at Doncaster in the batch of 'A4s' then on order, and wrote to Sir Ralph Wedgwood suggesting that this should be named *Sir Nigel Gresley*. Prentice received an acknowledgement almost by return of post, and when, over a year later, the naming ceremony of No 4498 took place, he received an invitation to be present. In later years some of the 'A4s' lost their bird names, in favour of names of directors or officers of the LNER, whilst another was renamed after Dwight D. Eisenhower, for whom Peppercorn had converted a sleeping car into an armour plated headquarters car during the war. Other 'A4s' received names appropriate to the 'Coronation' and the 'West Riding Limited' streamline trains, but once they had all been painted blue they tended to be used indiscriminately. The names given to other classes did not always show such inspiration. The 'Shires' broke no new ground (although it is difficult to understand the omission of 'Durham', the county in which they were all built, at Darlington) but to name engines after 'Hunts' was a novelty. Probably the suggestion came from one of the directors, amongst whom were several country landowners. The first batches of 'Sandringhams' were named after country estates, mainly in East Anglia, but although King George V and Queen Mary often travelled by train from Kings Cross to Wolferton, the station nearest to Sandringham, this duty was to be performed in the 1930s not by No 2800 itself, but by one of the two 'Super-Clauds' kept at Cambridge for the duty, No 8783 and 8787. *Cock o' the North* of course was another inspiration, and in a unique public relations exercise Boy Scouts were invited to suggest names for others of the class. 2,000 entries were received, and the winners were rewarded by a guinea and a trip round Doncaster Works. *Earl Marischal*, *Mons Meg* and *Thane of Fife* were submitted by the Scouts, as was *Maid of Glamis*, but this last name was evidently rejected as being too ladylike for such a masculine engine, *Wolf of Badenoch* sounding far more *puissant*. Often, official ceremonies took place when locomotive nameplates were unveiled. Photographs were taken, and eminent men invited to take the regulator for a short distance, as when the Hon Vincent Massey named No 4489 *Dominion of Canada*. Unfortunately he brought the engine to a stand beneath the Kings Cross station overbridge, and distinguished visitors standing nearby were covered in smuts.

The tradition of naming LNER Pacifics after racehorses was perpetuated throughout the postwar building of 'A1s' and 'A2s', although there were several exceptions. Edward Thompson and Arthur Peppercorn were commemorated by the first of their respective production series of 'A2s', and some fine Scottish names were chosen for some of the 'A1s', as well as wild birds displaced from 'A4s' on renaming. Eminent locomotive engineers from the GNR and NER were commemorated too, but not from the other constituent companies, so J. G. Robinson, among others, was omitted. W. P. Allen, a Great Northern driver, who became General Secretary of the Associated Society of Locomotive Engineers and Firemen (ASLEF) and finally a Member of the Railway Executive, gave his name to the first 'A1', No 60114, whilst four of this class joined *Great Northern* by recalling the main constituent companies of the LNER. Some of the names of the 'A1s' were suggested by members of the Railway Correspondence & Travel Society, and the final selection of names for this class was made in an orderly fashion by a committee of which George Dow, previously LNER Press Officer, was a member.

Two unofficial temporary renamings may perhaps be quoted. In 1944, at the request of Fitzherbert Wright, a member of the LNER Board, No 4486 was temporarily renumbered with the year of birth and given the Christian name of each of his three children. Only one side of the locomotive was specially treated, and it reverted to its original number and name as soon as photographs had been taken. In 1951, an 'A1' triumphantly bore the name 'Barnes Park' in chalk when returning to Leeds from Kings Cross on the day that the horse of that name had come home in the Lincolnshire Handicap at 33 to 1. The shed staff at Copley Hill had received a hot tip, and had done well out of it.

The 22 'Deltic' diesel-electric locomotives of 1960/1, which operated the main East Coast services until the coming of the Inter-City 125s, also received names. Originally they were all to be named after famous army regiments, the Chairman of the British Transport Commission at the time being General Sir Brian Robertson. However the Eastern Region Board, advised by Alan Pegler, demurred, and named their 'Deltics' after racehorses. This explains the curious mixture of regimental and racehorse names given to the class, but it is regrettable that many of the racehorse names were badly chosen and meant little to the travelling public. *Meld* and *Crepello* seemed particularly inapt. But the Gresley tradition commencing with the first to receive a racehorse name, No 4475 *Flying Fox*, in 1925, went through to No D9020 *Nimbus* in 1961.

The constituent companies of the LNER had adopted a variety of means of identification of locomotive classes. The North Eastern and North British followed a theoretically straightforward alphabetical system, under which each new class took the next letter in the alphabet, but there were several deviations from the strict rule. The Great Eastern gave a new class the works order number of the first batch to be built: thus the 'B12' 4-6-0s had been the GER Class S69. The Great Central system appeared completely arbitrary, consisting of a digit followed by a letter, as for example the LNER Class B7 4-6-0, which had been GC Class 9Q. On the Great Northern, Ivatt in 1901 introduced a letter/digit system which was continued by Gresley and applied by him to the LNER locomotive stock after grouping. The details were worked out by E. Windle of the Doncaster drawing office, types being denoted by 'A' (4-6-2), 'B' (4-6-0) and so on, the classes being identified by numerals. Subdivisions of the main classes were given a suffix. For example, the North Eastern 'S3' 3-cylinder 5ft 8in 4-6-0s were generically classed as 'B16'. Gresley's rebuilds became 'B16/2' (expressed as 'B16 part 2') and Thompson's version, 'B16/3'. The originals then took the classification 'B16/1'.

The system was inevitably complex, and there were several exceptions and irregularities, particularly in the application of the 'part' suffixes, but it had the great merit of a regular pattern, clearly identifying the many locomotive classes of the LNER. In this is possessed an advantage over the LMS and later BR practice of classifying locomotives by power rating rather than by wheel arrangement, which although perhaps a more logical basis failed to distinguish between different classes with the same power classification.

Chapter 14

Sir Nigel Gresley: an Appreciation

Nigel Gresley was not only a great locomotive engineer; he possessed a wide interest in mechanical engineering generally, and played a leading part in the proceedings of the Institution of Mechanical Engineers, and the Institution of Locomotive Engineers. He was elected President of the Mechanicals in 1936, and of the Locomotive Engineers in 1927 and again in 1934. In addition to his Presidential Addresses he read Papers and took part in discussions on numerous occasions, including meetings organised by other professional bodies. With Sir Henry Fowler he was joint author of a Paper given to the Civil Engineers in 1922, on the subject of Vacuum Brakes on Long Goods Trains, for which the authors each received a Telford Gold Medal. (In the Paper, Gresley described tests between Peterborough and Firsby during which 2-6-0 No 1646 hauled up to 101 8ton vans, demonstrating the feasibility of working such trains.) He also took part in discussions at the Institution of Electrical Engineers on electricity supplies to railways, and on the design of electric cooking equipment, having regard to its application to kitchen cars. However, he was not a prolific writer, and rarely contributed to technical journals; one interesting example was in 1929, when he wrote some notes for the 'Railway Gazette' in which he described a trip on a booster fitted CPR 2-10-4.

His Papers to the Learned Societies dealt with specific topics, and at no time, even in his Presidential Addresses, did he give a comprehensive review of his work. This had to wait until the very end of the LNER era, when A. H. Peppercorn gave permission for Bert Spencer and Norman Newsome to give Papers to the Institution of Locomotive Engineers describing respectively Gresley's locomotives, and his carriages and wagons. These two Papers, presented by men who for so many years were very close to Gresley, are still regarded as classics of their kind, giving details of many projects then unheard of outside the confines of the railway, and remain standard references for all students of LNER rolling stock practice. However, the subjects which Gresley dealt with in his addresses were all of importance, and included such topics as his philosophy concerning cylinders and valve gear, high speed trains, and high pressure locomotives. He also encouraged his staff to write and present their own Papers, as for example, Bulleid, on boosters and poppet valve gears, and Richards on the comparative economics of steam, electric, and diesel-electric traction.

One of Gresley's favourite topics was his strong desire to see the establishment of a national locomotive testing station, in which he echoed the thoughts of many of his contemporaries, demonstrating that whatever principles and prejudices he held, he was anxious to arrive at the truth, to discover, amongst the many conflicting aspects of locomotive design, what really were the best practices. He argued that, if locomotives could be tested away from the track under controlled conditions, the influence of such variables as coal, wind and the human factor, could be eliminated, and true comparative studies made and evaluated. He visualised the testing station as being a truly national institution, desirably as part of an independent scientific body such as the National Physical Laboratory. He opened the argument in his first Presidential Address to the Locomotive Engineers in 1927, and pressed the case in a Paper to the Mechanicals in 1931. His advocacy was such that the Board of Trade appointed a Committee to review the proposal; a favourable report resulted, but finance was not to be forthcoming from Government funds. This left the railway industry on its own, and of the four main lines and the manufacturers, only the LNER and LMS were fully in support. To the credit of both, agreement was reached in 1937 for the joint funding of the scheme. But because of the intervention of the war, the project was completed too late for Gresley, and indeed almost too late for the steam locomotive, as the Testing Station, at Rugby, was not opened until 1948. Had it been available during the heyday of steam, and, moreover, if the technology of the computer had been at the elbow of the designers, there might well have been greater commonality of design many years before British Railways. Many fallacies would have been exposed, the railways would have saved many thousands of pounds — but the rich assortment of British locomotive classes, good, mediocre, and sometimes downright bad, would have been greatly diminished, and later commentators and enthusiasts would have found much less to discuss.

Gresley's extra-mural activities were wide ranging, and took him well beyond the immediate railway scene. For example, following the loss of two steamships from what appeared to have been defective steering gear, Gresley, as an eminent engineer unbiassed by any previous association with marine matters, chaired a Board of Trade Committee to look into the question. In 1936, the Committee reported that the conventional rod and chain steering gear was satisfactory, but recommended a number of safeguards. Other Government work led to his membership of Ministry of Transport Committees on Automatic Train Control, and on Railway Electrification. Also, he took part in the activities of the British Standards Institution and its predecessor, the British Engineering Standards Association, particularly on mechanical engineering matters; in 1937 he was appointed to the General Council of the BSI. In the educational field, he was co-opted to the Governing Body of East London College, later Queen Mary College, from 1928 to 1939, as a person of eminence in the field of engineering.

He took an active interest in the work of the International Railway Congress Association, becoming a delegate to the Permanent Commission. Following the 1933 Session of the Congress in Cairo, he was invited to report on the organisation of the Egyptian State Railways workshops, whilst at the 1937 Session in Paris, he presented a report on 'Recent Improvements in Steam Locomotives', reviewing practice world-wide. He also visited Canada and South Africa, and he was a frequent visitor to France, developing a particular friendship with André Chapelon. Another facet of his professional life was his membership of the Association of Railway Locomotive Engineers. Founded in 1890, the ARLE provided an unofficial forum at which the Locomotive Engineers of the many railways of the period, and a few of the most senior asssistants, could meet together and discuss matters of mutual interest. Gresley became a member as soon as he was promoted to the position of Locomotive Engineer of the Great Northern, his proposer being J. F. McIntosh of the Caledonian, and his seconder Matthew Stirling (son of Patrick), of the Hull & Barnsley. Much of the discussion at ARLE meetings concerned matters of standardisation — for example, it was following a proposal by Gresley in 1918 that it was agreed that calculations of tractive effort should take a figure for boiler pressure of 85% of that rated; previously, depending upon the decision of the designer, percentages varied from 80 to 100%. Ironically, this acceptance of a standardised 15% pressure drop between boiler and cylinder led to an understatement of the tractive effort of many later LNER locomotives, when, following Gresley's work on streamlining internal steam passages, pressure drop was generally much less than this. However, when towards the end of World War 1, design proposals were promulgated for locomotives which might be adopted as standard, and used on several different railways, Gresley (and Raven) demurred. Although two of the proposed engines would not have been very different to his own 2-cylinder 2-6-0s and 2-8-0s (the GNR equivalents had considerably higher superheat), they were designed to a load gauge of 13ft 0in. The GNR load gauge was 13ft 6in above rail level and Gresley opposed standardisation of locomotives until standardisation of load gauges could be achieved. Evidently he did not wish to sacrifice the extra inches allowed him by the more generous GNR load gauge, although he did not always take full advantage of this, and in any case, after the grouping, the LNER were forced to adopt a maximum chimney height of 13ft 1in. His sense of authority emerges in the discussions at the ARLE at the time of the grouping. He was concerned that several locomotive engineers who would lose status under the grouping but who were senior in years, might achieve office in the Association and so lead to a situation in which a CME might be under the Presidency of one of his staff. This resulted in a formula in which the CME's became members of the Association, and nominated a small number of their senior assistants, the objective being that only a CME would become President. Gresley himself attained this office in 1926/7, during which period he improved the standard of meetings by encouraging members to submit papers for discussion. One such was by A. C. Stamer, on boosters, which was surprisingly critical, but Gresley indicated that he intended to pursue experiments with this device, now that he understood that these were to be made in Britain. Perhaps he had the North Eastern Atlantic conversion in mind at that time, whilst Stamer was not too keen.

In 1920, following the practice of most of his contemporaries, Gresley joined the Engineer and Railway Staff Corps, Royal Engineers, a military unit established to furnish advice to the Government on transportation matters. The Corps is remarkable in that its members do not wear uniform, perform no military duties, and receive no pay; it is entirely staffed by Officers of Field Rank and above. Gresley was commissioned as a Major, being promoted to Lieutenant Colonel in 1925, and continuing as a member of the Corps throughout the remainder of his life.

He was seldom far away from the work which he so obviously relished, and even his trips abroad were in the nature of busman's holidays. But he did not wrap himself up in his work to the exclusion of all other activities. Indeed he liked to live the good life of a country gentleman, particularly in his LNER days when friendship with Andrew K. McCosh led to shooting parties on the McCosh estate, Culter Allers, in Lanarkshire. This was relaxation which he obviously enjoyed, despite a damaged leg, the result in earlier years of an attempt by his brother to remove a thorn with a penknife; complications set in and almost led to amputation. He made a good recovery, as he enjoyed tennis and golf, whilst in 1928/9 he became Captain of Hadley Wood Golf Club, playing to a handicap of 12. Although never expressing a great interest in sailing, in the later 1930s he was Sir Charles Allom's guest on his yacht *White Heather* during Cowes Week.

His wife, née Ethel Fullagar died tragically of cancer in 1929; afterwards his elder daughter, Vi, was his constant companion until her marriage to Geoffrey Godfrey, son of Sir Dan Godfrey, the eminent musician, in 1937. They set up home at Watton-at-Stone, Hertfordshire, and Sir Nigel left his home at Salisbury Hall, near St Albans, to share their home at Watton, where his three grandchildren were born. Geoffrey Godfrey was a mechanical engineer, having been a pupil at Thornycrofts, and served throughout the war as an officer in the RAOC and REME. Following her father's death, Vi Godfrey did not wish to live at Watton on her own, and the house was let as wartime offices of the LNER. (Incidentally, Salisbury Hall, a Tudor mansion of historic interest, became the centre of design of the Mosquito bomber.)

Neither of Gresley's sons displayed their father's engineering genius, but both served with distinction during the war. His younger daughter, Marjorie, chose to follow a stage career, and her father was present at her debut at the opening night of Ivor Novello's 'Glamorous Night'. Illustrating his piquant sense of humour, perhaps not always apparent to more junior members of his staff, he visited her back stage at the end of the performance, saying how much he had enjoyed it, and added that the family's three pet dogs had been in the upper circle, and they had applauded, too!

Gresley's method of working, and his delegation of authority, were straightforward. Designs were discussed in outline in his office, but with attention given to important matters of detail. His own ability in draughtsmanship enabled him to explain points in such a way that a freehand sketch could be taken away and used almost as a scale drawing. He was constantly on the lookout for ways of improving locomotive efficiency but had to be convinced of the merits of any proposal before proceeding. He was receptive to ideas from his close associates, as well as keeping in touch with important developments wherever they might occur, and would consider carefully any well argued suggestions, accepting or rejecting them on the basis of good engineering practice. If he didn't like an idea, he explained why, and in this way gained the wholehearted support of his staff. He was a frequent visitor to the Drawing Office, and took a close personal interest in a developing design, even to talking over a point with a draughtsman engaged on some particular detail.

Nevertheless, he was sometimes slow to move, and was perhaps less receptive to suggestions from the running staff than he might have been, and did not take kindly to criticism of his engines. For example, a suggestion by E. D. Trask when Locomotive Running Superintendent, Scottish Area, that the 'P2s' might run more easily on the Aberdeen road if their driving wheels were flangeless was not given serious attention, whilst any attempted modification of locomotives at the sheds, particularly if unsuccessful, was robustly dealt with. 'Don't interfere with design', he said firmly. At the time of the 1925 exchanges with the GWR 'Castles' he was particularly sensitive to comments that the short travel valve gear of his Pacifics put them at a disadvantage. But when in their early days his first two Pacifics were encountering heating troubles in their main bearings, suggestions by W. A. Emerson, then District Locomotive Running Superintendent at Grantham, were warmly welcomed, as were later suggestions by Trask for improvements in the lubrication of small end bearings.

In all his designs, and in all his experimental work, he was anxious to make his locomotives more efficient converters of coal and water into energy at the drawbar; he was perhaps less concerned by the cost of maintaining them in good working order. He had been heard to argue that his engines needed good maintenance, and that he was entitled to expect this. But even during the days when labour was plentiful and cheap, maintenance was not all that could be desired, fitting staff being compelled to work in outdated and often appalling conditions. Possibly he would have modified his priorities had he been fully responsible for locomotive running on the LNER as he had been on the Great Northern, but the LNER decision to limit the span of management of the CME by excluding full responsibility for day to day locomotive maintenance in the sheds, whilst reasonable in that it enabled the CME's department to be better within the grasp of one man, introduced the inevitable disadvantage that the function of maintaining locomotives was divided between two Departments. The management situation was modified during the war, whilst with the worsening situation of the 1940s, had Gresley continued in office it is highly likely that circumstances would have forced a change of outlook, although hardly as radical as that of Thompson.

Like all great engineers, he possessed a strongly developed singlemindness of purpose, verging on autocracy, and once he had made up his mind to follow a particular course he was difficult to move away. He was a bold experimenter, and although relatively few of his experiments could be said to have been wholly successful, those which did succeed were outstanding. Moreover, he had the ability to see when an experiment was unsuccessful; he did not back failures. A not inconsiderable factor in his career was his ability to produce a series of well-proportioned locomotives during a long period of severe financial constraint, and when design on other railways was seldom as progressive as on the LNER. In particular, the introduction of the 'A4' Pacifics and the streamline trains reflected great credit not only on Gresley but on the LNER Board and the Chief General Manager of the time; a lesser team would not have possessed the imagination and initiative to bring these schemes to fruition.

Gresley's best memorial of course was his fleet of Big Engines, and the locomotive world is the poorer for not having had the opportunity to see more than the outline drawing of that massive 4-8-2. Perhaps he was too eager however to build a big engine for what he identified as a particular task without weighing the economics sufficiently carefully. More detailed investigation and analysis of operational considerations would have raised questions about the 'P1s', the Worsborough Garratt, and even the 'P2s'. Undoubtedly savings were made in engine crews (which may have induced a reaction from enginemen who did not agree), but it is problematic whether a realistic view was taken of all costs projected over the life of the locomotives. Nevertheless, whatever their viability, they were splendid examples of the locomotive builder's craft, to which their designer had contributed in such a unique way, from overall conception to influence on many of the details. Indeed, he went as far as to patent several of his innovations. These included the swing link pony truck, and double row superheater in 1913, conjugated valve mechanism (1916) and his feedwater heater and top feed arrangements seen in a few GN locomotives distinguished by an elongated dome. Later subjects were his corridor tender, and his idea of articulating locomotive and tender in conjunction with a booster, to be seen in the two rebuilt Raven Atlantics.

A number of Gresley locomotives have been preserved, notably *Mallard* and *Green Arrow* at the National Railway Museum, York, and *Flying Scotsman* and *Sir Nigel Gresley* which, in private ownership, remain on active service hauling steam specials from Steamtown, Carnforth. Those who have experience with operating these two Pacifics are well aware of their continuing capability. Richard Hardy, as a Doncaster trained engineer, can perhaps be forgiven for being enthusiastic, but Inspector George Gordon, who started with the LMS in 1935, cannot be said to possess any inbuilt bias in favour of a Gresley engine. Yet both speak in appreciative terms of the performance of Nos 4472 and 4498, even in comparison with *Duchess of Hamilton*, also at Carnforth. And George Hinchcliffe, Managing Director of Steamtown has told me 'sticking my neck out I believe that the "A4" is the best passenger steam locomotive ever built'.

In contrast to his work in 4ft 8½in gauge, Gresley's *Flying Scotsman* outline has been copied in smaller gauges, notably on the 15in gauge Romney, Hythe & Dymchurch Railway, whilst his Pacifics (and certain other classes too) form the subjects of many thousands of proprietary and scratch-built models.

Gresley's services were first recognised publicly in 1920 when he was appointed CBE for his work in connection with the war. In 1936 he was awarded the degree of Director of Science (Honoris Causa) by the University of Manchester, and later that year in the King's Birthday Honours, he was created Knight Batchelor.

As a final commentary on Sir Nigel Gresley, I would like to quote two men who knew him well. First, J. F. Harrison: 'He was admired and very greatly respected, having the natural ability to inspire confidence and enthusiasm. A visit from him was an inspiration.' And, from a letter written in 1941 by the LNER Assistant General Manager, Robert Bell, to Gresley's personal clerk, Harry Harper:

'Sir Nigel was a great man, forceful at times, but always kind at heart. He hated shirkers, but always put in a good word for those who put their backs into their work. He had a real affection for many of his people of all grades and positions. "Dear old so-and-so, what a grand foreman he was", he would say, or again he would speak of an old engine driver like Sparshatt who could generally get his engines to run well. If only our CME could have restrained his expenditure of energy he might have lived longer, but it is some consolation to know that he didn't outlive his powers. If he could not have gone on working he would have been miserable.'

Gresley developed a unique style of locomotive design and his influence in engineering matters was widespread. He was a man's man, a truly great engineer.

Acknowledgements
and Bibliography

The information contained in *The Gresley Influence* has been obtained from examination of original documents, and from interview and correspondence with many people who were close to Sir Nigel or who had experience with his locomotives. In particular I am indebted to J. F. Harrison OBE, T. C. B. Miller MBE, A. H. Emerson, T. Henry Turner, and E. D. Trask for their recollections, and to the doyen of LNER enthusiasts, W. B. Yeadon, for his generous help and guidance. I am deeply grateful to Mrs Vi Godfrey and to Miss Marjorie Gresley for their reminiscences of their father, and to Lord Garnock, President of the Gresley Society, for contributing the foreword.

Source material has been found mainly at the Public Record Office and at the Library of the Institution of Mechanical Engineers (S. G. Morrison, Librarian). C. P. Atkins, Librarian of the National Railway Museum, also gave valuable assistance, as did the Librarians of the Institution of Civil Engineers, the Institution of Electrical Engineers, and the Chartered Institute of Transport.

Other eminent engineers who have advised me include K. J. Cook OBE, E. S. Cox, whose technical guidance was invaluable, and T. Matthewson-Dick, whilst I am grateful too to M. G. Boddy, F. A. S. Brown, R. H. N. Hardy, N. Newsome, Col H. C. B. Rogers OBE, B. C. Symes and C. E. Whitworth, who gave me my first insight into LNER organisation. Particular aspects were dealt with by A. E. Beresford, W. Brown, B. C. Harding, R. G. Jarvis, Kaye McCosh, K. H. Leech, K. R. Prentice, R. W. Taylor and P. N. Townend. Other Institutions contacted included Marlborough College; the North Western Museum of Science and Technology; Queen Mary College; the University of London; the University of Manchester, and the Grammar School, Doncaster, where the Curator of the Railway Museum, H. Wilton Jones, was most helpful. Finally I must express my gratitude to my wife, Mary, for her patience in reading the text and making many pertinent suggestions, and for her assistance in typing draft and final versions.

For further reading, the student is referred to the following works, which have also been of help to me in the preparation of *The Gresley Influence.*

C. J. Allen; *The London and North Eastern Railway*; Ian Allan.

F. A. S. Brown; *From Stirling to Gresley*; Oxford Publishing Co.

F. A. S. Brown; *Nigel Gresley: Locomotive Engineer*; Ian Allan.

H. A. V. Bulleid; *Master Builders of Steam*; Ian Allan.

J. F. Clay and J. Cliffe; *The LNER 2-6-0 classes*; Ian Allan.

J. F. Clay and J. Cliffe; *The LNER 4-6-0 classes*; Ian Allan.

J. F. Clay and J. Cliffe; *The LNER 2-8-2 and 2-6-2 classes*; Ian Allan.

R. H. N. Hardy; *Steam in the Blood*; Ian Allan.

O. S. Nock; *The Gresley Pacifics*; David & Charles.

O. S. Nock; *The Locomotives of Sir Nigel Gresley*; Longmans.

H. C. B. Rogers; *Thompson and Peppercorn — Locomotive Engineers*; Ian Allan

J. W. P. Rowledge; *Heavy Goods Engines of the War Department*; Vol 1; Springmead Railway Books.

P. N. Townend; *Top Shed*; Ian Allan.

Loco Profiles:

    1 *LNER non-streamlined Pacifics*.

    14 *Pennsylvania Pacifics*.

    19 *Gresley A4s*.

    Profile Publications.

Locomotives Illustrated:

    20 *Gresley Eight-coupled Locomotives*.

    25 *Gresley A1/A3 Pacifics*; Ian Allan.

and in particular

Locomotives of the LNER the comprehensive and very detailed work published in a numbers of Parts by the Railway Correspondence & Travel Society.

Finally, readers who desire to keep alive the memory of Sir Nigel Gresley are recommended to become members of the Gresley Society by writing to the Hon Membership Secretary.

Index

158